The

EVERYTHING KIDS'

Math Puzzles
Book

Brain teasers, games, and
activities for hours of fun

Meg, Glenn, and Sean Clemens

Adams Media Corporation
Avon, Massachusetts

EDITORIAL
Publishing Director: Gary M. Krebs
Managing Editor: Kate McBride
Copy Chief: Laura MacLaughlin
Acquisitions Editor: Bethany Brown
Development Editor: Julie Gutin
Production Editor: Khrysti Nazzaro

PRODUCTION
Production Director: Susan Beale
Production Manager: Michelle Roy Kelly
Series Designer: Colleen Cunningham
Layout and Graphics: Paul Beatrice,
Colleen Cunningham, Rachael Eiben,
Daria Perreault, Erin Ring, Frank Rivera

An Everything® Series Book.
Everything® and everything.com® are registered trademarks of F+W Media, Inc.

Published by Adams Media, a division of F+W Media, Inc.
57 Littlefield Street, Avon, MA 02322 U.S.A.
www.adamsmedia.com
ISBN 13: 978-1-58062-773-3
ISBN 10: 1-58062-773-0

Printed by LSC Communications, Harrisonburg, VA, US

20

November 2016

This publication is designed to provide accurate and authoritative information with regard to the subject matter covered. It is sold with the understanding that the publisher is not engaged in rendering legal, accounting, or other professional advice. If legal advice or other expert assistance is required, the services of a competent professional person should be sought.

— From a *Declaration of Principles* jointly adopted
by a Committee of the American Bar Association and a Committee of Publishers and Associations

Many of the designations used by manufacturers and sellers to distinguish their products are claimed as trademarks. Where those designations appear in this book and Adams Media was aware of a trademark claim, the designations have been printed in initial capital letters.

Cover illustrations by Dana Regan.
Interior illustrations by Kurt Dolber,
with additional illustrations by Barry Littmann and Kathie Kelleher.
Puzzles by Beth Blair.

Puzzle Power Software by Centron Software Technologies, Inc. was used to create puzzle grids.

This book is available at quantity discounts for bulk purchases.
For information, call 1-800-289-0963.

See the entire Everything® series at *www.everything.com*.

Contents

Brain Benders / 83

Probability Puzzles / 95

Random Remainders / 105

Introduction

As math teachers, we often hear these complaints: "I just can't do math" or "Math was never my thing." Sometimes it's students who are frustrated in class; other times it's parents who can't help their kids with math homework. In the latter case, parents may unintentionally pass on their own fear of math to their children.

Although we certainly understand that math comes more easily to some than to others, we believe anyone can "get it" and *should* get it. It's very important that all kids learn math because it will be an essential skill in the twenty-first century. The puzzles in this book will help kids develop skills in arithmetic, geometry, number sense, logical thinking, and problem solving, which form the foundation of mathematical understanding.

Math is more than just a collection of math facts and vocabulary (although those are important). Math should also be a way of thinking about and solving real problems. You can be an absolute whiz at the multiplication tables, but you won't find them very useful if you are unsure when you

should be multiplying and when you should be dividing. Here is a simple everyday-life problem: There are forty-five fifth-graders going on a class trip to the Museum of Math Puzzles. Parent volunteers with minivans are driving; each van can carry six students. The teachers plan to have enough cookies on the trip for each student to get four. How many cookies do the parents need to prepare and how many vans should they take? If your answer is eight vans and 180 cookies, your field trip will be a success.

Math puzzles are both fun and rewarding—we are confident that any child will enjoy doing the puzzles in this book, and knowing that you've solved a challenging puzzle is definitely rewarding. Beyond simple enjoyment and satisfaction, puzzles also provide wonderful opportunities for learning. Challenging puzzles offer children a chance to practice skills they already know and also to stretch their minds and extend their knowledge by discovering new ideas.

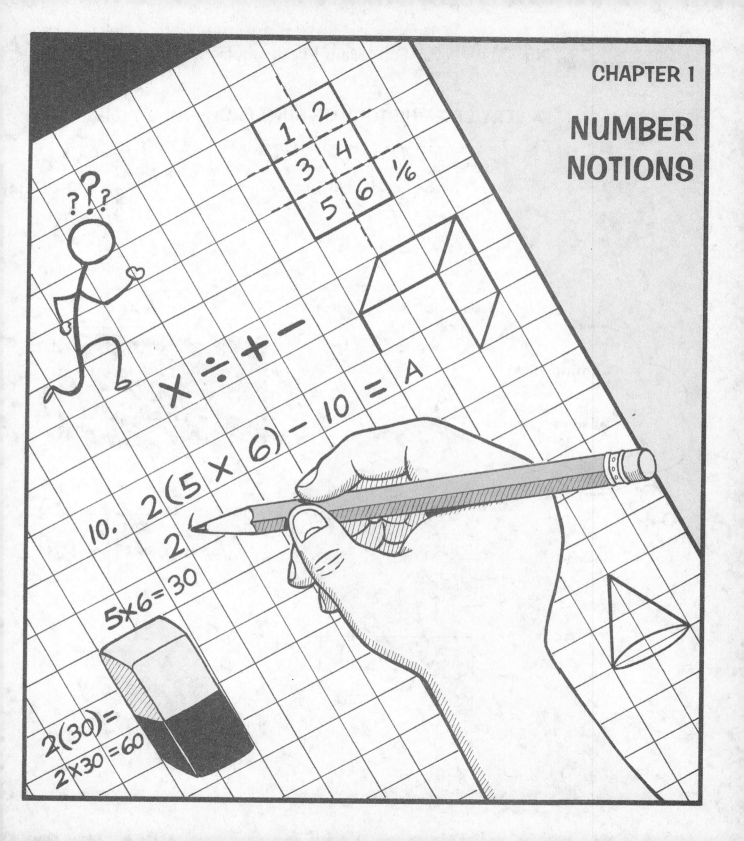

CHAPTER 1

NUMBER NOTIONS

"uhn"

"uhn uhn"

A VERY BRIEF HISTORY OF NUMBERS

No one knows who invented numbers, but it's fun to think that some early caveman named Oog did it when he said "uhn," "uhn uhn," and "uuuuuuhhhn," which meant "one," "two," and "lots."

Tallying

The earliest written numbers were most likely **tallies**—simple lines that each represent one object. You have probably used them yourself to keep score in a game with a friend:

You: / / / / /
Friend: / / / / / / /

Counting Sticks

Tallies were found carved on pieces of animal bone about 50,000 years old. What do you think those people were counting?

Roman Numerals

The Roman numerals, invented by—yes, you guessed it!—the Romans, served many people over many centuries, and have not been forgotten today. Can you think of how they might be used?

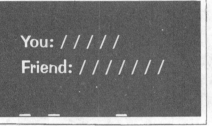

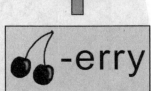

ROMAN NUMERALS

number	Roman numeral
1	I
5	V
10	X
50	L
100	C
500	D
1,000	M
5,000	$\overline{V}$
10,000	$\overline{X}$

FUN FACT

It's about Time!

Today, Roman numerals are most often used to show time (see if you have a clock in your house that uses Roman numerals) and dates (try to find Roman numerals on old buildings and also in movies and videos).

HEE HEE HEE

The rules for reading the Roman numerals sound difficult but are actually very simple, once you get the hang of it:

I. When a symbol is followed by a smaller symbol or symbols, you add up their values.

For example: VI = 6; CXXIII = 123; DII = 502.

II. When a symbol or symbols are followed by a larger-value symbol, you subtract their values:

For example: IV = 4; CMXL = 940; CDII = 402.

So, the numbers for 1, 2, 3, 4, 5, 6, 7, 8, 9, and 10 are I, II, III, IV, V, VI, VII, VIII, IX, and X. Are you beginning to catch on? If so, see if you can handle the following puzzles.

What do you call a person who can't stop doing sums?

An add-ict !

Figure This Out

Which face would you see on a grandfather clock?

Grandfather clocks use Roman numerals for each hour, but with a surprise: Four o'clock is represented with IIII instead of IV! See if you can find a watch with Roman numerals on its face and check out four o'clock.

▶ Try This
Read All about It!

Want to practice your Roman numerals? How about counting a thousand squealing pigs? Just grab *Roman Numerals I to MM* by Arthur Geisert (Houghton Mifflin Company, 1996) and let the fun begin. We'll bet you never knew there could be so many pigs in one picture!

When in Rome

Question:
What would you use to count organic apples?

First, take a look at these Roman numerals and see if you can figure out what numbers they represent.

a	b	e	l	m
XIV	XXIX	VIII	LXI	CDXI

n	r	s	t	u
CXLIX	MDCVI	DCCLI	MMDCLX	CMXXII

Now, place the letter for each Roman numeral under the corresponding Arabic number to find the answer to the puzzle.

Answer:

149	14	2660	922	1606	14	61

149	922	411	29	8	1606	751

Adding and subtracting with Roman numerals is not easy; and multiplication and division are nearly impossible.

XLIII + XXIV = ____________________ (LXVII)
XCII – XXVI = ____________________ (LXVI)
XV × IV = ____________________ (LX)
XVIII ÷ III = ____________________ (VI)

WORDS 2 KNOW

digit: A number—but also a word for "finger." Coincidence? We think not. It's very likely that the first people to start counting used their fingers—just as little kids continue to do today.

Arabic Numerals

To simplify things, people eventually gave up Roman numerals in favor of the Arabic system, which relies on ten digits—0, 1, 2, 3, 4, 5, 6, 7, 8, and 9.

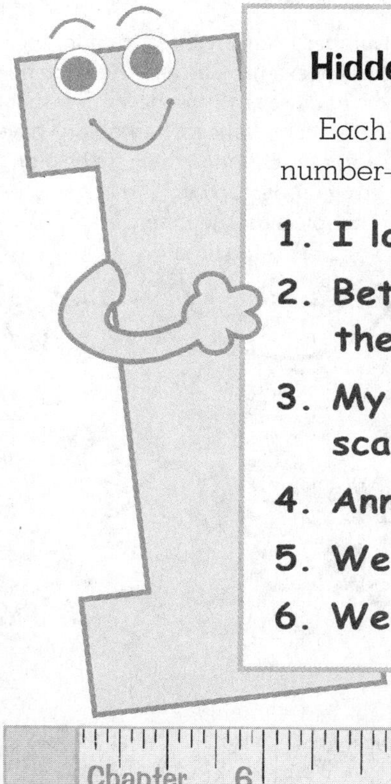

Hidden Numbers

Each of the following sentences has at least one hidden Arabic number—circle as many as you can find!

1. I love my computer—when it works!
2. Beth reeked of smoke after sitting by the campfire.
3. My mother likes to weigh tomatoes on every scale in the store.
4. Annie was even early for school last week!
5. We can stuff our dirty backpacks in your tent.
6. We like the mirrored maze room at the fun park.

Practice Your Digits

Get from START to END by moving around the square either vertically (up or down) or horizontally (left or right), moving the number of squares given by the number you are on. (For example, if you are standing on 3, you can move three spaces up, down, left, or right.)

START 3	3	4	2	3
4	1	1	2	2
2	4	3	1	4
2	3	1	4	3
4	2	1	2	END E

START 4	2	1	2	3	4
3	3	4	2	3	4
4	2	4	2	4	3
3	2	1	3	2	4
2	2	4	2	3	4
4	1	4	1	2	END E

THE IMPORTANCE OF ZERO

How important is "nothing"? Sometimes, it's very important. But we humans didn't always understand what exactly "nothing" is.

We need zero for several reasons. For one thing, how can you tell what's 15 − 15? Furthermore, we need zero as a placeholder. Otherwise, how would you tell the difference between 5 and 50, or between 25 and 205?

"You're just nothing without me!"

"You're worth ten times as much when you're with me!"

Counting Sheep

Numbers were invented to count things. For example, an early herdsman might have wanted to know how many sheep he had. If he had no sheep, he wouldn't have wasted his time counting them, so he didn't need a number for them—that's why people didn't need zero for a long time!

What's 10 + 8 - 3 + 12 - 7 - 5 - 15 ?

A whole lot of work for nothing!

ALL YOU NEED IS 0 AND 1

What does math really fast and always gets the right answer? No, it's not that smart kid at school—it's the computer. Computers don't have anything like fingers. Instead, early computers had simple circuits that act sort of like ordinary light switches—they turn on (1) and off (0). So computers do all their math by just using zeros and ones. This is known as a binary system.

How does the binary system work? Well, it's all about the number placement and the powers of 2. Each place *n* in the sequence that is "turned on" (marked with 1) stands for a 2 raised to the power *n*:

BINARY SYSTEM	
binary number	Arabic numeral
0	0
1	1
10	2
11	3
100	4
101	5
110	6
111	7
1000	8
1001	9
1010	10

$$1 \ (2^0) \quad 2 \ (2^1) \quad 4 \ (2^2) \quad 8 \ (2^3) \quad 16 \ (2^4) \quad 32 \ (2^5) \quad 64 \ (2^6) \quad 128 \ (2^7) \ldots$$

So, a binary number 110 is actually $2^2 + 2^1 + 0$, or $4 + 2 = 6$.

On or Off?

What time is it when the math teacher goes to the dentist? Convert the binary numbers to find out.

Number Decoder

H	6
I	3
O	8
R	2
T	7
Y	10

111	1000	1000	111	110	-
___	___	___	___	___	-
111	110	11	10	111	1010
___	___	___	___	___	___

3.14159265358

A NUMBER WITH A NAME

Now you see that we just can't live without zeros. But there is another special number that is very important in mathematics. That number is π (pronounced the same as "pie"), and it represents the ratio of the circumference of a circle to its diameter: what you get if you divide the distance around the circle (circumference) by the distance across the circle (diameter).

WORDS 2 KNOW

mathematics: Based on the Greek word *manthanein* (to learn), mathematics measures and describes the world with numbers and symbols.

How Close Were They?

In 1957, Pegasus computer calculated π to 7,840 decimal places. And in 1967, CDC 6600 broke a record by giving us π to 500,000 decimal places. Can you imagine how much paper would be necessary just to print out this number?

What's surprising to many people is that the answer turns out to be the same for any circle, no matter how big or small it is.

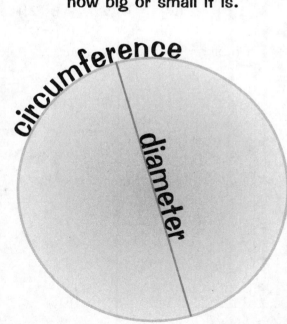

circumference

diameter

A Slice of π

You can approximate the value of π with some string, a ruler or yardstick, and a calculator. Search your home for circular objects of different sizes: a cup, a large jar, a bicycle tire. For each item, find its circumference by wrapping the string around it and then measuring the string. Then find the diameter by measuring across the widest part. Then divide the circumference by the diameter.

Because no one can measure perfectly, you will not get the exact same answer each time. But you should find that π is around 3.1 to 3.2 no matter what size circle you measure.

FUN FACT

The European Way

In the European decimal notation, decimals and commas are switched. A decimal is used to separate groups of thousands and a comma is used between the units' place and the tenths' place. For example, the number 1,234.56 is written as 1.234,56. This has confused plenty of Americans in Paris!

HEE HEE HEE

People knew about π for a long time, but they had trouble trying to figure out its exact value. Here are a few examples:

- **Ancient Babylonians estimated π to equal 3.**

- **Ancient Egyptians thought it to be 3.1605.**

- **An ancient Greek named Archimedes estimated π to be between $3^{10}/71$ and $3^{1}/71$.**

- **In China 1,500 years ago, Tsu Ch'ung Chi measured it to be $355/113$.**

- **A great Arab mathematician, al-Khwarizmi, calculated π to be 3.1416.**

Consequently, mathematicians continued getting more precise, until humans got some help from computers.

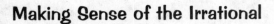
Making Sense of the Irrational

The value of π has fascinated people for centuries. Mathematicians and ordinary people alike have spent years looking for patterns in the digits. Do some digits appear more frequently than others? **Count up how many times each digit appears below and see if you can detect a pattern.**

Here are the first 201 digits of π:

3.1415926535....8979323846 2643383279

5028841971 ......6939937510......5820974944

5923078164......0628620899 8628034825

3421170679 ......8214808651 3282306647

0938446095 ....5058223172......5359408128

4811174502........8410270193 8521105559

6446229489 5493038196

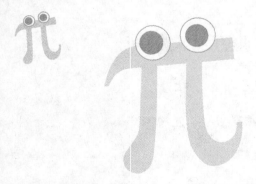

WORDS 2 KNOW

irrational: To many people, **irrational** means foolish or even crazy, and maybe that's how you are feeling about π about now! Well, mathematicians agree, but for a different reason. In mathematics, irrational numbers are those that cannot be represented as a fraction—they go on forever and ever with no repeating pattern.

digit	tallies	total
0		
1		
2		
3		
4		
5		
6		
7		
8		
9		

Now, you can graph the results on the facing page to see if a pattern emerges.

DIGIT VALUE

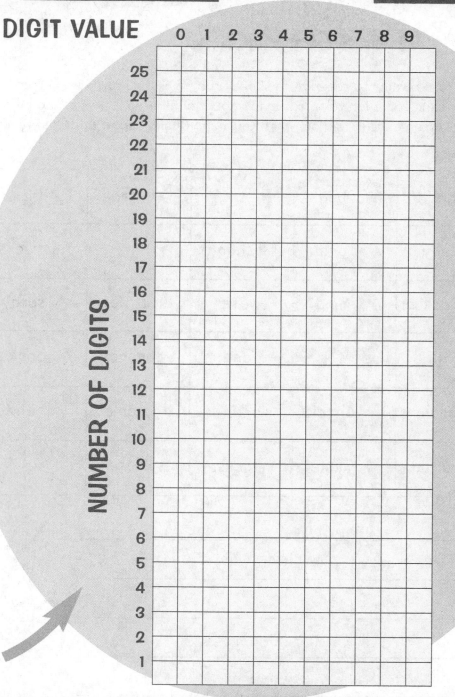

DIGIT VALUE

0 1 2 3 4 5 6 7 8 9

NUMBER OF DIGITS

25 24 23 22 21 20 19 18 17 16 15 14 13 12 11 10 9 8 7 6 5 4 3 2 1

Let's Get Packing

In the space next to the word box (or on a separate sheet of paper) list all the words in the boxes with the number 1. Then do the same for the words in the boxes numbered 2, 3, 4, 5, and 6. Finally, write each list of words as a sentence to find out **what Kayla and Dustin had to do to get ready for their hiking trip.**

1 Call	4 and	2 bug	1 to	5 extra	2 block
4 bottles,	1 Kelly	5 and	3 flashlight	6 Find	4 snacks,
2 Buy	5 Pack	6 bird	4 water	1 directions	2 spray.
3 the	4 Fill	1 for	6 and	5 ponchos	6 books.
1 Short	6 binoculars	3 Check	2 sun	3 batteries.	2 and
4 chocolate!	1 park.	4 make	5 socks.	1 State	4 get

1. _____

2. _____

3. _____

4. _____

5. _____

6. _____

See What I Mean?

You usually add and subtract by writing numbers on a piece of paper, or using a calculator. But there are other ways to talk about numbers. For example, people who know **American Sign Language** can use hand signals! Study the chart below. Then write the answer to each sign language equation in number form. **See if you can sign the answer, too.**

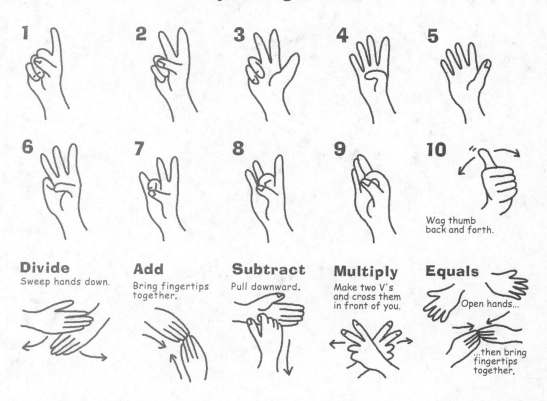

1 **2** **3** **4** **5**

6 **7** **8** **9** **10**
Wag thumb back and forth.

Divide
Sweep hands down.

Add
Bring fingertips together.

Subtract
Pull downward.

Multiply
Make two V's and cross them in front of you.

Equals
Open hands...
...then bring fingertips together.

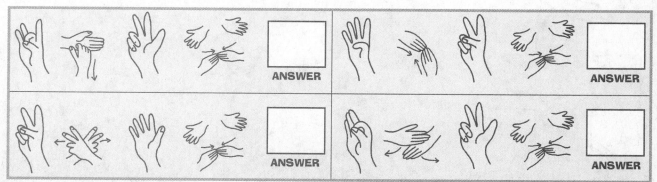

ANSWER

ANSWER

ANSWER

ANSWER

NOTES

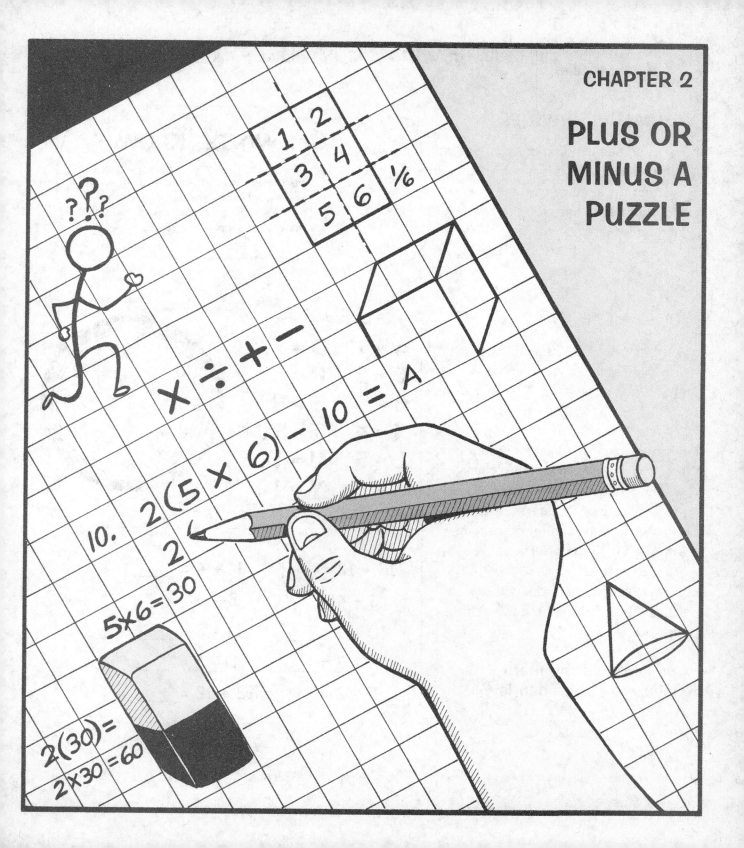

ARITHMETIC ACTIVITIES

Arithmetic is doing calculations with numbers, especially addition, subtraction, multiplication, and division. If you already know most of your basic arithmetic facts, you are ready to try the following activities and puzzles.

WORDS 2 KNOW

calculate: This term originated from the Greek word *kalyx*—pebble or small stone—because a long time ago, Greeks used small stones to do simple calculations.

Clock Math

Arithmetic is full of surprises! Don't believe it? Try this question on a friend: When does **10 + 4 = 2?** He'll probably think you are crazy, but you're not. This question has a perfectly sensible and important answer: **When it is 4 hours after ten o'clock.**

Adding and subtracting on a clock doesn't always work the same way as adding and subtracting regular numbers. Use the clock to solve the following problems. Then use the decoder and the numbers in the shaded boxes to figure out the answer to this riddle:

What time did the math teacher go to the dentist?

Decoder

A = 1	O = 7
C = 2	R = 8
H = 3	S = 9
I = 4	T = 10
L = 5	U = 11
M = 6	Y = 12

10 + 12 = _____

3 + 4 = _____

10 + 9 = _____

1 - 3 = _____

5 - 2 = _____

11 + 4 = _____

8 + 3 = _____

11 - 3 = _____

11 - 1 = _____

12 + 12 = _____

Calendar Math

Here is another practical arithmetic problem. When does 5 + 3 = 1? Three days after the fifth day of the week: from Thursday (5) to Sunday (1).

It doesn't really make sense to say "Thursday + 3 = Sunday," but if you give each day of the week a number, then you can do calendar arithmetic exactly as you did clock arithmetic. The trick is, if your result is over 7, just subtract it from the total. In our example, 3 + 5 = 8; 8 – 7 = 1. Now, what day is 12 days after a Wednesday? 4 + 12 = 16; 16 – 7 = 9; 9 – 7 = 2. This means that 12 days after Wednesday is a Monday—two weeks from then.

Sunday = 1
Monday = 2
Tuesday = 3
Wednesday = 4
Thursday = 5
Friday = 6
Saturday = 7

"The different branches of Arithmetic— Ambition, Distraction, Uglification, and Derision."

—Lewis Carroll, Through the Looking Glass

When Numbers Don't Obey

Why don't hours of the day and days of the week work the same way as "normal" numbers? Maybe it has to do with limits. Normally, numbers go up as far as infinity, so you never have to start over. With defined terms like the day (which can never have more than twenty-four hours) or the week (which can never have more than seven days), you can't go on forever and therefore need to start over, which messes up the calculation. Can you think of any other instances when numbers don't behave normally?

NUMBERS WITH DIRECTION

Recall that numbers were originally used to count things, like sheep, and it took centuries before a symbol was invented to represent zero.

Are there any numbers that are <u>less</u> than zero?

Today, most people have heard of negative numbers, and know that they are not at all imaginary and are really quite useful. Think of where you may have heard of numbers like –5 and –10. Did you think of a thermometer? Negative numbers represent temperatures below 0 degrees (those are the cold days, whether you use a Fahrenheit or Celsius thermometer).

For every "positive" number, there is its twin "negative," and vice versa. These pairs are called "opposites": 3 and –3; –12 and 12; 135,000,789 and –135,000,789.

Using a simple number substitution (A = 1, B = 2, C = 3, and so on), figure out the coded word below to get the name of a useful math tool that will help to show you negative numbers and how they work.

14	21	13	2	5	18

12	9	14	5

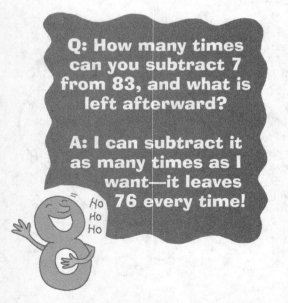

Q: How many times can you subtract 7 from 83, and what is left afterward?

A: I can subtract it as many times as I want—it leaves 76 every time!

Ho Ho Ho

Adding Signed Numbers

Why would we want negative numbers? One reason is that mathematicians don't like problems that have no answer. Everyone knows that we can add any two numbers, say 5 + 3. Most people also know that in addition, the order of the numbers doesn't matter. The answers to 5 + 3 and 3 + 5 are the same.

Now let's try subtraction: 5 – 3 is no problem; everybody gets 2. But what if we switch the numbers? What is 3 – 5? Is it still 2? Think of what subtraction means. If you have five pieces of candy and give three to your little brother (very generous of you!), then you have two pieces left. But if you have three pieces of candy and give five to your little brother . . . hey, wait a minute, you can't do that! And if you could, you sure wouldn't have two pieces left! So at least with candy, 3 – 5 doesn't make any sense; there is no answer.

Mathematicians really hate that. If you can do 5 – 3, you ought to be able to do 3 – 5. So what is the answer? To find out, we use a **number line.** Notice that if you pick any number on the number line, all the numbers to its left are less than it while all the numbers to its right are greater.

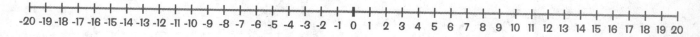

Adding 5 + 3 on the number line is easy. You start at the 5, and then count three more spaces to the right and see where you end up (which is always on 8, since 5 + 3 = 8). Note that starting at the 3 and counting five spaces to the right gets you to the same place (3 + 5 = 8). Subtracting is just as easy. To do 5 – 3, you start at the 5 and count three spaces to the left.

Now, what about 3 – 5? After you pass 0, you get to –1 (one less than zero), –2 (two less than zero), –3 (three less than zero), and so on—we use a negative sign in front of the number to show numbers that are to the left of zero on the number line. If you move five spaces to the left of 3, you get to –2. So 3 – 5 = –2. Now, what about 2 – 7? If you got –5, you are on the right track!

FUN FACT

Hard to Believe!

Even after mathematicians began thinking about negative numbers, numbers that are less than zero, many of them called such numbers "fictitious," "imaginary," or "useless."

HEE HEE HEE

The Bottom Line

Can you come up with the rules for adding and subtracting positive and negative numbers? Here is a summary:

- Add a positive number by moving right.
- Add a negative number by moving left.
- Subtract a positive number by moving left.
- Subtract a negative number by moving right.

But wait—there's more! You can actually add and subtract using negative numbers as part of the problem, instead of just the answer. Try these:

$$7 + (–5) = \underline{\quad}$$

$$–4 – (–7) = \underline{\quad}$$

Did you figure out how to do it, or does it look totally impossible? Once you know the rules, it's really easy. Just keep thinking about the number line. If you see a +, you are counting to the right. If you see a –, you need to count to the left.

Let's do $7 + (–5)$ first. This is an addition problem, which means you need to count from 7 to the right. However, because the second number is negative, you actually have to switch directions and count five spaces to the left. That means $7 + (–5) = 2$.

The same approach should work for $–4 – (–7)$. Start at –4. Subtraction means moving to the left, but since the second number is negative, we do the opposite and move right seven spaces, so $–4 – (–7) = 3$.

Connect the Dots

Solve the following addition and subtraction problems using the number line. As you solve each problem, connect to the dot with the correct answer. Start with the dot labeled **START +** and do all the addition problems. Then, pick up the pencil and move to the other 0 that is labeled **START –** and do the subtraction problems.

Do in order	Addition	Subtraction
A.	-3 + -5 =	-3 - -5 =
B.	-4 + 2 =	4 - -8 =
C.	-1 + 5 =	5 - 2 =
D.	4 + -8 =	- 4 - -2 =
E.	7 + -2 =	7 - -2 =
F.	-3 + 3 =	-2 - -2 =
G.	3 + 4 =	-3 - 4 =
H.	-2 + -2 =	-1 -1 =

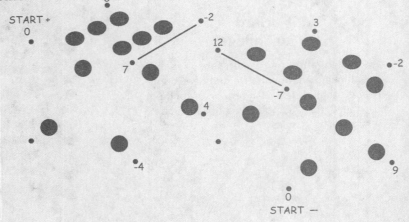

MAGIC SQUARES

Magic squares have been popular math puzzles for over 3,000 years, and once were thought to have mystical powers. Follow these simple rules to complete your own magic square:

1. Use each number only once.
2. Each row, column, and diagonal must add up to the same answer.

FUN FACT

Historical Squares

Over 3,000 years ago, ancient Chinese included magic squares in their mystical writings. Magic squares also appeared in art. For instance, Albrecht Dürer's famous engraving of *Melancholia* (1514) includes a picture of a magic square.

HEE HEE HEE

For this first magic square, use the numbers from 1 to 9. HINT: Each column, row, and diagonal adds up to 15.

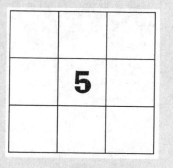

Try again, but this time use only the EVEN numbers from 2 to 18 (2, 4, 6, and so forth). HINT: Each column, row, and diagonal adds up to 30.

Try again, but this time use only the ODD numbers from 1 to 17 (1, 3, 5, and so forth). HINT: Each column, row, and diagonal adds up to 27.

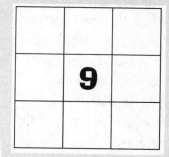

Now, let's make things more difficult. In the following magic square, some of the numbers are negative—you need to use every number from –4 to 4. HINT: Each column, row, and diagonal adds up to 0.

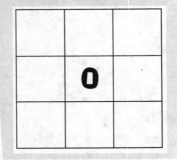

Here is another magic square. This time, use the numbers from 3 to 5. HINT: Each column, row, and diagonal adds up to 3.

How Big Can You Go?

If you think the 4-by-4 square is hard, you'll really be impressed by Ben Franklin, a scientist, inventor, statesman, printer, philosopher, musician, and economist (a jack of all trades!), famous for flying a kite during a lightning storm. In addition to all his other jobs and hobbies, Ben liked to solve math puzzles. One of his mathematical achievements was to solve an 8-by-8 and 16-by-16 magic square. That's humongous! Visit *www.pasles.org/ Franklin.html* to take a closer look at Ben's magic squares.

So, now you think you are a magic square pro? Not so fast! Let's make the magic square larger and see if you can still solve the puzzle. For the following square, use the numbers from 1 to 16. HINT: Each column, row, and diagonal adds up to 34.

16			13
4			1

GAME OF 15

Here is another **add**ictive game you can play! All you need is another player, a piece of paper, and a pen.

First, write down the numbers 1 through 9 on a sheet of paper, like this:

1 2 3 4 5 6 7 8 9

Then, you and another player take turns selecting numbers. When a number is selected, the player who chose it crosses it off the list and it can no longer be taken. The first person to get *any* 3 numbers that add up to exactly 15 wins!

For example:

Player #1 picks 5
Player #2 picks 8
Player #1 picks 6
Player #2 picks 3
Player #1 picks 1
Player #2 picks 7
Player #1 picks 9—and wins

Player #1 wins because
1 + 5 + 9 = 15

Try Playing Game of 15 Yourself!

To distinguish who picked which numbers, Player #1 can cross off the numbers by marking an X over it and Player #2 can circle the numbers he or she picks.

1 2 3 4 5 6 7 8 9

1 2 3 4 5 6 7 8 9

1 2 3 4 5 6 7 8 9

SOLVE A CROSS-NUMBER PUZZLE

You have probably seen crossword puzzles, and it's possible that you have even solved one or two yourself. But what about cross-number puzzles? Does it sound like something you'd like to try? The cross-number puzzle in this chapter is special. In order to solve it, you have to read the following story for clues, so pay attention!

The Camping Trip

There was an old lady who lived in a shoe. She had so many children she didn't know what to do.

Well, one day, she just couldn't stand it anymore. Jamie was fighting with Orville, Wilbur wanted a snack, Oscar and Ophelia were drawing crayon pictures on the walls, and Hortense was crying because Delphinia had stolen her *Math Puzzles* book. And it was just seven o'clock in the morning.

"Enough already!" shouted their mother, "I need some peace and quiet. All of you, play outside for the rest of the day. Better yet, canoe over to Mystery Island and play there. Even better, make it a camping trip! Yes, everybody go camping on Mystery Island. Don't come back until Christmas."

At first this seemed rather harsh but then everybody remembered that Christmas was just two days away. This got the children, who had been quiet for just a moment, all excited again. "Out!" yelled the mother.

The children immediately began preparations. With three kids to a canoe, they needed a dozen canoes and two paddles for each canoe. Each kid grabbed clean underwear, two extra pairs of socks, exactly four pounds of food and fifteen pounds of equipment (bowls, cups, silverware, sleeping bags, flashlights, handheld video games; Hortense took along her *Math Puzzles* book).

At eight o'clock in the morning, they piled into the canoes and paddled out to Mystery Island. The trip took just three-quarters of an hour and was uneventful until they had almost reached the island. Jamie was leaning out over the edge of her canoe when she said, "Hey, we're in canoe number 29."

"No, you're not," laughed Gertrude from another canoe. "You're reading it upside down!"

"I am?" asked Jamie, and tried to twist around to see it right and promptly fell in the lake. "Yeow!" she shrieked, while splashing hurriedly to shore, "this water is FREEZING!"

Jamie quickly got out of her wet clothes and crawled into her sleeping bag from where she could supervise the setting up of the tents. Originally, the kids wanted to sleep three to a tent, but they didn't have enough tents so they crowded in four to a tent. Five of the tents were just enough for the boys, the others were for the girls. Unfortunately, no one had remembered to bring tent pegs, so the rest of the morning was spent scrounging up pieces of wood until there was enough for twelve pegs for each tent. The kids then ate a hearty lunch of chocolate-chip cookies.

The next order of business was to build a fire, which wasn't easy because so much of the available wood had been used for tent pegs. Things weren't looking too hot until Rupert brought over a big piece of wood, broke it in half, and fed it to the fire that immediately started burning much better. All the kids cheered except Dominic who yelled, "Rupert, you dodo, that was a canoe paddle!"

The afternoon was spent exploring the island, playing games, fishing, and talking about what everyone hoped to get for Christmas. Jamie stayed in her sleeping bag all afternoon, playing solitaire and waiting for her clothes to dry by the fire. She didn't win many solitaire games after the wind blew her cards around and the Seven of Hearts landed in the fire.

Dinner was more cookies, toasted over the fire this time; after that, the children all sat around telling ghost stories. This was great fun until Mabel, with big eyes, said quietly, "Uh, guys, I think I hear something creeping around in the woods!"

Instantly, everyone was quiet and all ears were listening for noises. After a few minutes, they all heard a distinct "whooo-oo-oo." Immediately, everyone ran for the tents and dove into their sleeping bags and didn't come out until morning.

The next day, Lysander got a length of rope and tied knots in it every seven feet to make it easier to hold on to. He ended up with nine knots, including one at each end. The children spent the morning making up different teams and waging tug-of-wars with Lysander's rope until it broke. Later in the day, some of them held a fishing contest. Maxwell won by catching the most fish. Penelope caught half as many as Maxwell, Guineviere caught a third as many as Penelope did, and Baxter caught one-quarter as many as Guineviere. Baxter's fish was so small that he let it go. No one else caught anything. That night, they had a fish feast.

The next morning, all the children were up early and eager to get home. But they were short one canoe paddle and no one was sure what to do about it until Xavier suggested they tie all the canoes together end to end and make a big "supercanoe." The canoes were each eight feet long and when they were all tied together bow to stern they were hard to control. The supercanoe was veering left and right, like a huge water snake, as the kids tried to cross the lake. Nevertheless, the kids made it home in one hour, arriving at 8 o'clock in the morning. Their mother, well rested, was delighted to see them back and they all celebrated a great Christmas. (Except their neighbor Fergus, who insisted for many years after that he had seen a sea serpent on the lake that Christmas morning.)

Now you can try to solve this crossword puzzle using the clues you read in the story . . .

Across

1. Number of campers on the trip
3. Date on which they returned home
5. Total length of the supercanoe
6. Total number of canoes plus tents
8. How many minutes it took to get home
9. Total number of hours the trip lasted
10. Number of paddles on way home
11. Total number of fish caught during the contest
12. Length of Lysander's rope (before it broke)
13. Total weight of food and equipment in each canoe (pounds)
15. Number of hours from noon to midnight

Down

1. Water temperature, according to Jamie
2. Jamie's canoe number
3. Number of girls on the trip
4. JAMIE on the telephone
7. Total number of tent pegs needed
10. Total number of socks on the trip
11. Number of minutes it took to get to the island
13. Number of cards left in Jamie's deck
14. Number of ears that listened for ghosts

A Puzzle of Your Own

Did you like the story and the cross-number puzzle? Maybe you can create one for your friends or family to solve. You can be as inventive as you like—to provide clues, make up a story, provide word problems, or simply give clues that the puzzle solver is likely to know.

Cross Sums

You must figure out what combination of numbers to use so that each column or row adds up to the totals shown in the white numbers. The white arrows show you in which direction you will be adding, and we have left you some numbers as hints. Better sharpen your pencil!

Here are a few simple rules:

- You are only adding the numbers in any set of white boxes that are touching each other.
- Use only the numbers 1 through 9. Each number can only be used *once* in each set.

Remember, you need to think ahead a little bit. Each number has to be correct both across and down!

WORDS 2 KNOW

Fibonacci series: A series of numbers that begin with 1, 1, 2, 3, 5, 8, 13, and so on, where the two first numbers add up to the third (1+1=2), the second and third numbers add up to the fourth (1+2=3), and so on. This sequence was devised by Leonardo Pisano (Fibonacci), a mathematician who lived in Pisa, Italy, between 1170 and 1250.

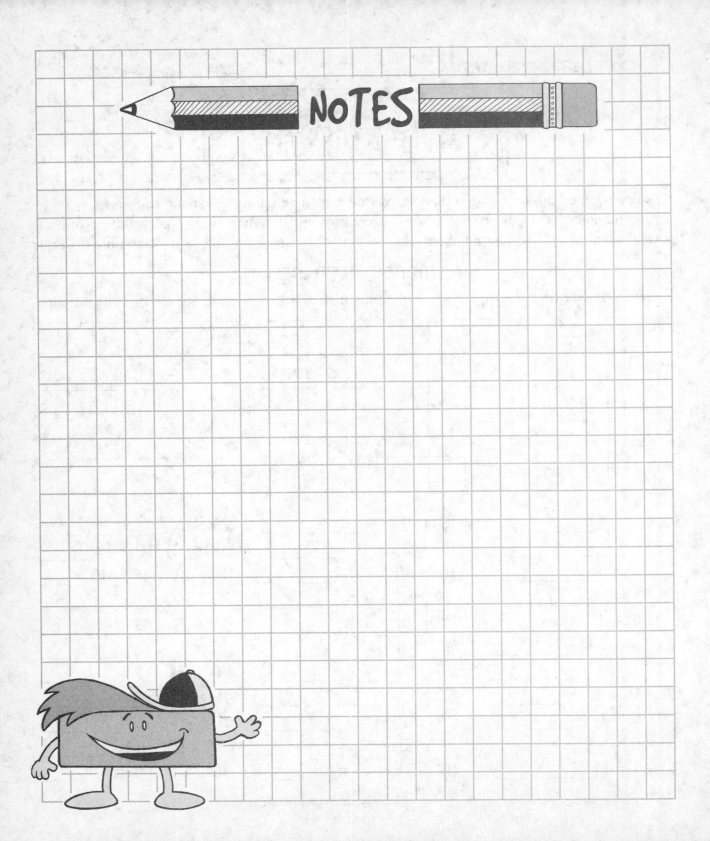

NOTES

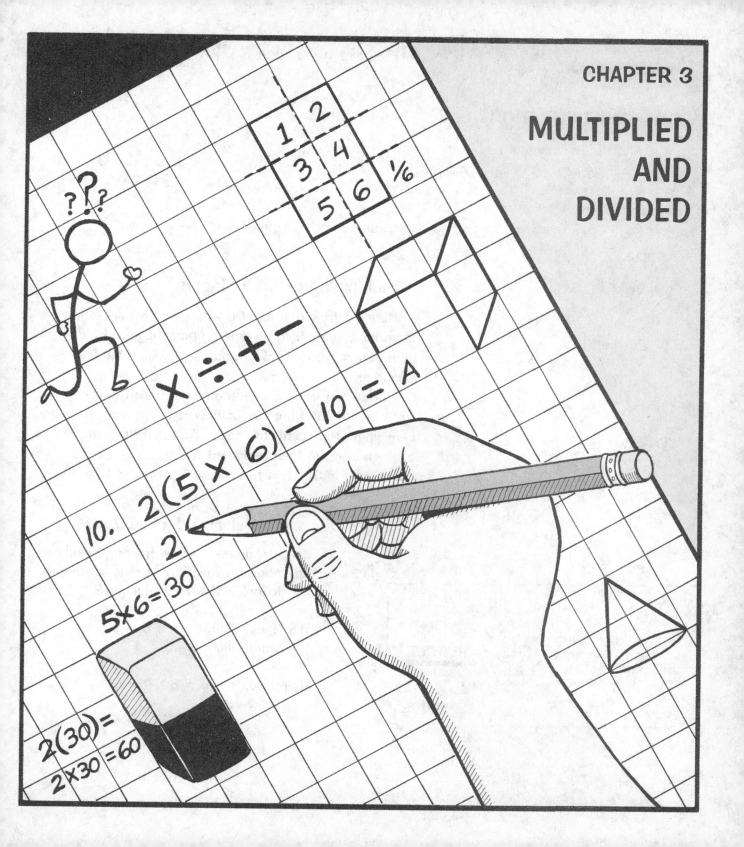

CHAPTER 3

MULTIPLIED AND DIVIDED

MIGHTY MULTIPLICATION

Multiplication is nothing more than a shortcut to addition. Let's say you have five baskets with apples, and each basket contains seven apples. If all you know is addition, you will have to do the following problem: $7 + 7 + 7 + 7 + 7$. Or, if you know how to multiply, you can just do 7×5. Either way, you will get the same number of apples: 35.

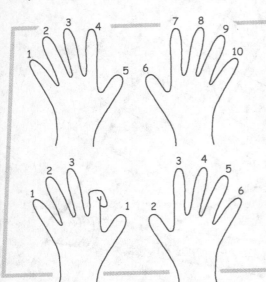

Multiplying on Your Fingers

Here's a trick you can try with your friends—show them how to multiply by nine on your fingers. Hold your hands out in front of you. Then follow the following example.

To multiply 4×9, bend down the fourth finger from the left. The number of fingers to the left of the bent finger represent the "tens" digit and the number of fingers to the right represent the "ones" digit, so the answer is 36. This trick works up to $9 \times 9 = 81$.

• To Multiply 9 by Any Digit •

Can you figure out how the finger multiplication trick works? Here is another way to look at it—try to multiply 9×6:

The "tens" digit: $6 - 1 = 5$
The "ones" digit: $9 - 5 = 4$

Therefore, $9 \times 6 = 54$. Right?

Play Five in a Row

Improve your multiplication skills by playing Five in a Row, a game of multiplication tic-tac-toe, at *http://nu.fi.ruu.nl/wisweb/en/applets/html/00023/welcome.html*.

Russian Peasant Multiplication

In Russia, peasants used to use an interesting technique for multiplication—**halving, doubling, and adding numbers.** When you have two numbers that you need to multiply, keep doubling one as you divide the other in halves (ignore any remainders or fractions). If the number in the halved column is odd (including the original value), mark the doubled number for addition later. At the end, add all the marked doubled numbers. Sounds complicated? It will make a lot more sense with an example. Let's take 22 × 44.

HALVE THIS COLUMN	DOUBLE THIS COLUMN	MARK THE DOUBLED NUMBERS WHERE THE HALVED NUMBER IS ODD
22	44	
11	88	+
5	176	+
2	352	
1	704	+
Sum = 968		

In the first column, there are three odd numbers: 11, 5, and 1. Their corresponding doubles are 88, 176, and 704; 88 + 176 + 704 = 968. So, 22 × 44 = 968. If you don't believe this, check by using your calculator!

◀ How about trying one for yourself? Try using the Russian peasant method to multiply **25** by **34.**

HALVE THIS COLUMN	DOUBLE THIS COLUMN	MARK THE DOUBLED NUMBERS WHERE THE HALVED NUMBER IS ODD
25	34	
Sum =		

Practice ChisenBop

ChisenBop is an ancient method of doing basic math using your fingers. Kids who are good at ChisenBop can add and subtract as fast as a calculator! Check out *http://klingon.cs.iupui.edu/ ~aharris/chis/chis.html* for pictures and lessons.

Positive and Negative Numbers

In Chapter 2, you learned how to add and subtract positive and negative numbers. But what about multiplication? Do the same rules apply? Actually, they don't. In fact, the number line method doesn't work for multiplication. Instead, it might be helpful to imagine a video of a person who is walking backward and forward. People can walk backward and forward, and the video can be played forward or rewound:

> **Walking forward is a positive action.**
> **Walking backward is a negative action.**
> **Film running forward is positive.**
> **Film running backward is negative.**

Imagine that you videotape your friend walking forward. If you watch it on video played forward, you will see your friend walking forward. This represents multiplying two positive numbers: **(+) × (+) = +.** Now, if you rewind the tape, your friend will seem to be walking backward: **(+) × (–) = –.**

Now imagine you videotape your friend walking backward and then play the video forward. On the screen, you will see your friend walking backward: **(–) × (+) = –.** But what if you took that same film and played it backward? It would appear that your friend is actually walking forward:
(–) × (–) = +.

FUN FACT

To Make a Long Story Short

The nice thing is that these exact same rules work for division, so you needn't learn any more new rules. In fact, these four rules are usually shortened to make them easier to remember: For multiplication and division, if the signs are the same, the answer is positive. If the signs are opposite, the answer is negative.

Multiplication Boxes

Now you are ready for some fun with multiplication boxes. A multiplication box has six multiplying problems: Each row and each column are separate problems; the first two numbers are multiplied to get the third number.

The following multiplication box is filled out for you, with explanations on the side and bottom.

-3	4	-12
2	-6	-12
-6	-24	144

-3 x 4 = -12
2 x -6 = -12
-6 x -24 = 144

-3 × 2 = -6
4 × -6 = -24
-12 × -12 = 144

Now, complete each of the following multiplication boxes:

-4	5	
-9		
	30	

7	10	
		-11
	-10	

		21
-5		10
	-6	

-3		-18
-21		1008

DAUNTING DIVISION

Which arithmetic operation is the most difficult? Most people think it's division. Problems like 42 ÷ 7 = 6 are not too bad; you just memorize them. Hopefully, you already have your division facts memorized or maybe you are working on them now in school. Problems like 542 ÷ 7 are harder. You have to learn how to solve them.

WORDS 2 KNOW

obelus: The symbol "÷" used to indicate division. The word comes from the Greek word *obelos*, for spit or spike, a pointed stick used for cooking. The symbol has been used as a division symbol since around 1650.

One of the things that makes division difficult is that unlike addition and multiplication, even when you start with two whole numbers, the answer is not always a **whole number;** it may be a **decimal** (for example, 43 ÷ 8 = 5.375). This is different from adding or multiplying. When you add or multiply any two whole numbers, your answer is always another whole number—no exceptions. Mathematicians say that whole numbers are **closed** for addition and multiplication.

Musical Math

Use division to complete the ten problems. Then cross off the answers in the box below. The remaining letters will spell out the answer to the following riddle:

What comes before a tuba?

Y	A	U	O	R	N	Y	M
31	45	47	16	19	12	21	29
R	E	B	R	M	G	A	W
44	13	15	33	25	18	22	14

$5\overline{)95}$ $4\overline{)72}$ $3\overline{)87}$ $6\overline{)84}$

$7\overline{)175}$ $3\overline{)141}$

$8\overline{)168}$ $6\overline{)264}$

$8\overline{)264}$ $6\overline{)186}$

Divisibility Rules

So, is there any way to tell whether a division problem is going to work out to a whole number? Yes, there is. There is a set of rules called Divisibility Rules that tell whether the answer to a division problem will be a whole number without actually having to do the long division.

 Dividing by 1: If you divide any whole number by 1, you always get a whole number.

 Dividing by 2: Even numbers "evenly" divide into 2. Odd numbers divide into 2 with an "odd one out."

 **Dividing by 3:** Add up the digits (twice, if necessary); if the sum is divisible by 3, then the number is too. Let's say you need to divide 123: $1 + 2 + 3 = 6$, which is divisible by 3, so 123 is divisible by 3. Another example: 678678. Add $6 + 7 + 8 + 6 + 7 + 8 = 42$; $4 + 2 = 6$, which is divisible by 3. That means 678678 is divisible by 3.

 **Dividing by 4:** Look at the last two digits. If they are divisible by 4, the number is as well. For example, the last two digits of 2357924 are 24, which is divisible by 4. Therefore, 2357924 is divisible by 4.

 **Dividing by 5:** If the last digit is a 5 or a 0, then the number is divisible by 5. For example, 2357925 is divisible by 5, because the last digit is a 5.

 Dividing by 6: If the number is divisible by both 3 and 2, it is divisible by 6 as well. For example, 2157924 is divisible by 6 because it is even (divisible by 2) and the digits add up to 30, which is divisible by 3.

 **Dividing by 7:** To find out if a number is divisible by 7, take the last digit, double it, and subtract it from the rest of the number without the last digit. If you get an answer divisible by 7 (including 0), then the original number is divisible by 7. If you don't know the new number's divisibility, you can apply the rule again. For example, 161 is divisible by 7 because 2×1 (the last digit) = 2 and $16 - 2 = 14$, which is divisible by 7.

Dividing by 8: If the last three digits of a number are divisible by 8, then so is the whole number. How do you check the last three digits? If the first digit is even, and the last two digits are divisible by 8, the number is divisible by 8. If the first digit is odd, subtract 4 from the last two digits; the number will be divisible by 8 if the resulting last two digits are. For example:

- **2448:** Check the last three digits, 448. Here, 4 is even and 48 is divisible by 8, so 2448 is also divisible by 8.
- **192:** Here, 1 is odd, so you need to subtract 4 from the last two digits: 92 − 4 = 88; 88 is divisible by 8, so 192 is as well.

Dividing by 9: Add the digits. If they are divisible by 9, then the number is as well. For example: 52866 is divisible by 9 because 5 + 2 + 8 + 6 + 6 = 27, and 27 is divisible by 9.

WORDS 2 KNOW

solidus: The slanted bar "/" used for fractions and division. During the Roman Empire, the solidus was a gold coin. On the reverse of the coin was a picture of a spear bearer, with the spear going from lower left to upper right. This spear became the symbol for fractions and division.

A Problem with No Answer

There is one case in which division is not allowed. Do you know what it is? Try the following problem: 2 ÷ 0. Since division is the opposite of multiplication, this is the same as asking, "What number times 0 will equal 2?" Any number multiplied by 0 is equal to 0, so it's impossible to have a number that, when multiplied by 0, will equal 2. That's why 2 ÷ 0 really does have no answer. Division by 0 is simply not allowed.

Dividing by 10: If the number ends in 0, it is divisible by 10.

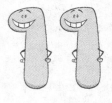

Dividing by 11: Keep subtracting the last digit from the previous digits until you can tell if the resulting number is divisible by 11. For example: 645634 is divisible by 11 because 64563 − 4 = 64559; 6455 − 9 = 6446; 644 − 6 = 638; 63 − 8 = 55, and 55 is divisible by 11.

Dividing by 12: Check for divisibility by 3 and 4.

Stepping Stones • Your goal is to cross the river on stepping stones. Each time you need to take a step, roll two dice and add the numbers. Use the divisibility rules to find a stepping stone that has a number divisible by your dice roll and place your marker on the stone (you and your partner should use different sets of markers—if you use pennies, your partner can use nickels or dimes).

Take turns rolling the dice and placing a marker. **The first person to connect a line of markers (including along a diagonal) from one bank of the river to the other wins!**

270	1386	350	396	308	720	1056
990	336	864	1000	770	432	990
495	1155	297	1188	512	220	243
210	162	1001	840	363	1320	144
315	576	504	693	360	660	1331
168	1260	280	440	729	1440	1500
792	594	441	252	462	924	972

PRIME NUMBERS

Let's see. Prime beef is the best beef, so prime numbers must be the best numbers, right? Well, maybe prime numbers are not the best, but they are very important.

You can probably figure out the first several prime numbers in your head. But as the numbers get bigger, it gets harder to know if they are prime (quick, is 91 a prime number?). For thousands of years, people have been curious about ways to find prime numbers. **The Greek mathematician Eratosthenes invented one such way more than two thousand years ago.**

WORDS 2 KNOW

prime number: A number that is divisible by just two different numbers, 1 and itself. Seven is prime because it can only be divided by 1 and 7. Eight is not a prime number because besides 1 and 8, it is also divisible by 2 and 4. The word **prime** comes from *primus,* the Latin word for "first."

Is 1 a Prime Number?

Most mathematicians do not consider 1 to be either a prime or a composite number. It is a special number in multiplication because you can multiply any number by 1 and the answer is the same. Because of this property, 1 is called an **identity for multiplication.**

The Sieve of Eratosthenes

The Sieve of Eratosthenes is a method for finding prime numbers on a number grid, and you can try it yourself by working with a **number grid.** • First, circle the 2, then cross out all the numbers that are multiples of 2. • Then, circle the next number not crossed out, 3, and cross out all numbers that are multiples of that number. • Continue to circle the number closest to the beginning and cross out all its multiples until all the numbers are circled or crossed out. • When you are done, the circled numbers are **prime** numbers and the crossed-out numbers are **composite** numbers.

Who's That?

Eratosthenes (276–194 B.C.) was born in Cyrene, North Africa (now Libya), and died in Alexandria, Egypt. He was a well-rounded scholar who investigated many areas of math and science. He estimated the circumference of the Earth to be about 24,400 miles. Now we know it's about 24,900 miles—Eratosthenes was remarkably accurate for his time.

	2	3	4	5	6	7	8	9	10
11	12	13	14	15	16	17	18	19	20
21	22	23	24	25	26	27	28	29	30
31	32	33	34	35	36	37	38	39	40
41	42	43	44	45	46	47	48	49	50
51	52	53	54	55	56	57	58	59	60
61	62	63	64	65	66	67	68	69	70
71	72	73	74	75	76	77	78	79	80
81	82	83	84	85	86	87	88	89	90
91	92	93	94	95	96	97	98	99	100

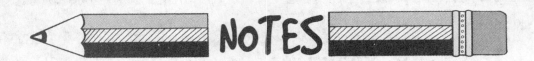

NOTES

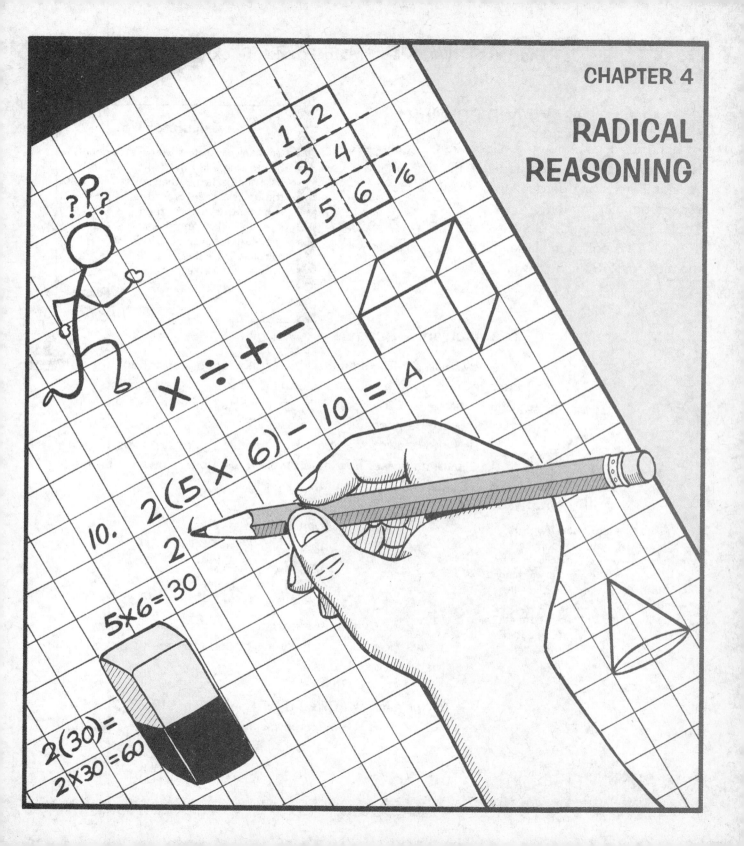

CHAPTER 4

RADICAL REASONING

GROWING BY LEAPS AND BOUNDS

In the previous chapter, you learned that multiplication is simply repeated addition. But did you know that there is an operation that substitutes for repeated multiplication?

Here is an example: $3 \times 3 \times 3 \times 3 \times 3 = 3^5 = 243$. The **3** here is called the **base**, the **5** is the **exponent**, and the answer, **243**, is the **power**.

A Calculator Tip

On many calculators, you use exponents by pressing a key marked x^y. Put in the base number first, 3, then press the x^y key, then press the exponent value, 5, then press the = key. You should see 243 as the answer. (A few calculators use the symbol $\wedge$ instead of the x^y key.)

The Allowance Scam

You may have heard about the famed allowance scam that made a few lucky math-wiz kids into millionaires—at their parents' expense. Here is how it works: Tell your parents that you are willing to accept two pennies for your allowance, but with one catch. Every day, the allowance should be raised to the next power. **If your parents agree, how much money will your allowance be by the end of the month (in thirty days)?**

It's Growing and Multiplying!

As you may have noticed with the allowance example, exponents on whole numbers can quickly lead to some very large answers. Many things in both nature and people's lives (though probably not your allowance) grow by repeated multiplication instead of repeated addition. Such growth is called **exponential growth**.

Day 1	$2^1 = 2$
Day 2	$2^2 = 4$
Day 3	$2^3 = 8$
Day 4	$2^4 = 16$

If you continue receiving your payments for thirty days, how much will you be entitled to receive on the last day of the month?

2^{30} pennies = 1,073,741,824 pennies or $10,737,418.24 —over ten million dollars!

SQUARES AND RADICALS

Square numbers are numbers that are the result of multiplying the same number twice. In other words, they can all be written with the exponent 2:

$$1^2 = 1, \ 2^2 = 4, \ 3^2 = 9, \ 4^2 = 16, \ 5^2 = 25, \ 6^2 = 36, \ldots$$

You can see what square numbers look like when you look at floor tiles, like the ones you probably have on the bathroom floor.

$1 \times 1 = 1^2 = 1$ $2 \times 2 = 2^2 = 4$ $3 \times 3 = 3^2 = 9$ $4 \times 4 = 4^2 = 16$

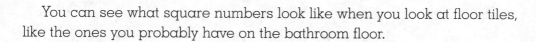

Complete the table to find more square numbers.

5^2	=	25	13^2	=	
6^2	=		14^2	=	
7^2	=		15^2	=	
8^2	=		16^2	=	
9^2	=		17^2	=	
10^2	=		18^2	=	
11^2	=		19^2	=	
12^2	=		20^2	=	

Goofy Gardener

Use the decoder to figure out the answer to this riddle:

Why did the mathematician plant his garden in milk cartons?

A   E   O

G   Q   R

S   T   U

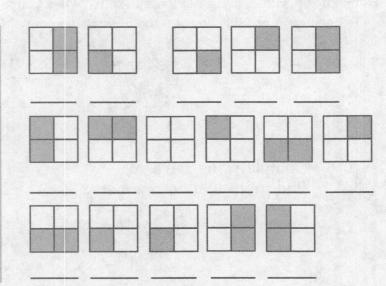

A Radical Sign

You know that subtraction is the opposite of addition and division is the opposite of multiplication. The operation called **squaring** also has an opposite, called the **square root.** A square root of a number is written using a **radical sign:** $\sqrt{36}$ means "What number must I square (multiply by itself) to get 36?" If you know your multiplication facts, you should be able to find an answer fairly easily—it's 6, because $6 \times 6 = 36$. Now that you know what a square root means, finish filling in the following table.

$\sqrt{1}$	=	1	$\sqrt{36}$	=	6
$\sqrt{4}$	=	2	$\sqrt{}$	=	7
$\sqrt{9}$	=		$\sqrt{64}$	=	
$\sqrt{}$	=	4	$\sqrt{}$	=	9
$\sqrt{25}$	=		$\sqrt{100}$	=	

The Square Root's Double

Did you know that $\sqrt{36}$ has another square root in addition to 6? Can you think of what it is? What other two identical numbers can you multiply to get to 36? How about -6×-6? All positive numbers really have two square roots that are opposites of each other, one positive and the other negative.

On Your Mark!

Answer each equation with a number between 1 and 10. Then read the phrases in order (read the number, too!) from least to most to find a popular way to count to the beginning of a race!

$\sqrt{9}$ ___ to get ready,

$-3+4$ ___ for the money,

2^2 ___ to go!

$4 \div 2$ ___ for the show,

FUN FACT

Drawkcab (Backward) Numbers

Palindromes are words that read the same forward and backward. "Racecar" is a palindrome. Numbers can be palindromes if they are the same forward and backward, like 121. Here's how to make your own palindrome numbers:

- Start with any number: 49
- Reverse it: 94
- Add the two: 49 + 94 = 143
- Reverse the sum: 341
- Add again: 143 + 341 = 484

Presto! You've got a palindrome number: 484.

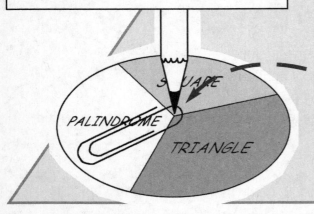

THREE IN A ROW

This is a game for two players. The goal of the game is to identify SQUARE, TRIANGULAR (divisible by 3), and PALINDROME numbers and be the first player to get three of your markers in a row. To play, you will need:

- A paper clip
- A pencil
- Two sets of different place markers (such as coins, buttons, or small candies)

Use the point of a pencil to hold one end of a paper clip at the center of the spinner and spin the paper clip.

A Never-Ending Jar

An ancient Chinese porcelain jar has a sea, an island, two countries each with three mountains, and so on in *Anno's Mysterious Multiplying Jar* by Masaichiro and Mitsumasa Anno (Philomel Books, 1983). See how factorials can represent the total number of mountains and much larger numbers!

Q: When is a number not real?

A: When it is imaginary.

Ho Ho Ho

Square

Triangular

Palindrome

Player 1 spins the paper clip and places a marker on a number in the grid that matches the category picked (for instance, if the paper clip lands on "square," Player 1 can place a mark on 4, 9, 16, and so forth). Then, Player 2 does the same. Players take turns to see who can get three of their markers in a row first.

HINT: Some of the numbers fit more than one category.

1	105	99	49	21	88
3	16	11	22	25	55
100	111	91	77	9	15
4	101	78	66	6	44
64	10	242	141	121	33
81	45	28	131	36	144

How Four Can You Go?

Four is a very powerful number. With exactly four fours (4 4 4 4), you can make lots of other numbers. Using addition, subtraction, multiplication, division, and square roots, as well as some parentheses (to show what to do first), see if you can come up with the numbers from 1 to 15. We've done 1 as an example, but feel free to do it again—most of these can be done more than one way.

1 =   EXAMPLE: $4 \div 4 + 4 - 4 = 1$

2 =

3 =

4 =

5 =

6 =

7 =

8 =

9 =

10 =

11 =

12 =

13 =

14 =

15 =

HINT: Stumped? Don't forget that $\sqrt{4} = 2$!

Your Number's Up

See how many common phrases or familiar objects you can think of that relate to the following numbers. Can you fill in all the blanks? We did a few to get you started.

1	16
2	17
3 LITTLE PIGS	18
4	19
5	20
6	21
7	22
8	23
9	24 HOURS IN A DAY
10 FINGERS OR TOES	25
11	50
12	100
13	
14	
15	

★ If you are stumped, you can check the answer key, but don't be surprised if your answers are different than ours!

NOTES

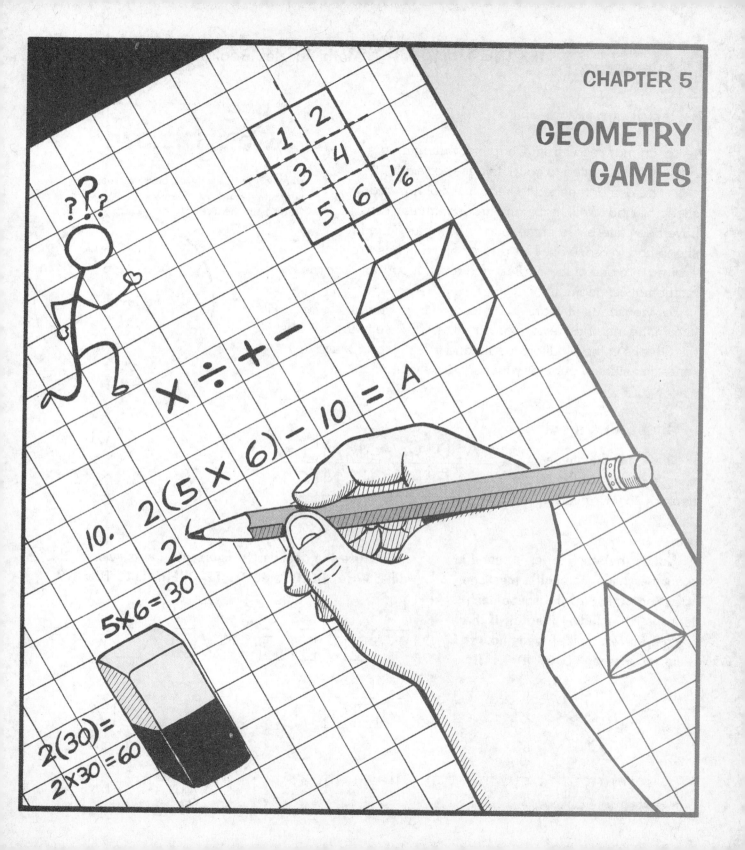

AN ANCIENT MATH

You may recall from Chapter 1 that numbers were invented to count things—for example, a herdsman needed to keep track of how many sheep he had. Well, that same herdsman may also have been interested in measuring how much land his sheep had to graze on. This and other problems like it evolved into one of the earliest and most important branches of mathematics: geometry.

For thousands of years, many people from around the world have known the importance of geometry. The Chinese in the Far East, the Greeks in the Mediterranean, and the Inca and Maya in the Americas studied geometry thousands of years ago.

WORDS 2 KNOW

geometry: A study of physical shapes. Literally, **geometry** means "to measure the Earth."

Shape Changers

These are the shape-change codes for the puzzle you are about to solve.

A	D	G		J	M	P
B	E	H		K	N	Q
C	F	I		L	O	R

S / T / W
T / V / X / Z
U / Y

Notice that each letter is found in a unique shape. To send a message, draw the outline of the shape each letter is in, including the dot, if there is one. For example, here is how to send the message **LOOK AT THAT!**:

L O O K   A T   T H A T !

Now use the decoder to figure out the answer to this riddle: **WHAT DO GEOMETRY TEACHERS LIKE TO EAT?**

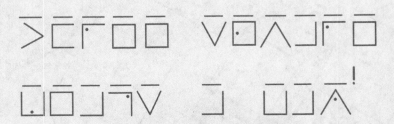

Chapter 1 2 3 4 5

BASIC GEOMETRY

Understanding geometry requires learning lots of words that are used to describe geometric figures and properties. Some of them you will encounter here. Although you won't begin your studies in geometry until high school, you already know a lot of geometrical concepts. You can tell the difference between a long line and a short line or between a square and a circle, and you already know about π (Chapter 1).

Six-Sided Math

Here are four big hexagons that share some edges with each other. Use the numbers from 1 to 9 to fill in the empty spaces. When the puzzle is finished, the six numbers around every big hexagon should add up to 30.

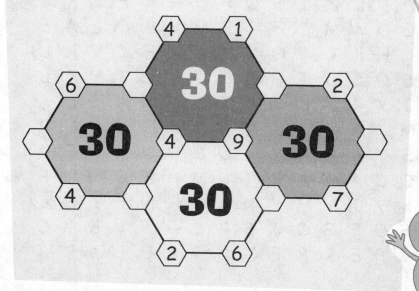

WORDS 2 KNOW

polygon: A geometrical figure with three or more sides. The term **polygon** is from the Greek roots *poli* (many) and *gonus* (knees). Greeks thought of a polygon as a shape of many angles, which look like bent knees.

Q: Why did the cube cross from the second to the third dimension?

A: The second dimension was too square.

Ho Ho Ho

Hide in Plain Sight

See if you can find this list of basic geometry terms hidden in the letter grid.

HINT: The words in the grid will be "acting out" their meaning. For example, if you were searching for the word CIRCLE, expect to find the letters in a circular pattern, not a straight line! This means that some of the words will appear more than once in the puzzle, even if they only appear once in the list!

EXTRA CREDIT: Use bright-colored markers to run a line through each word you find. If you use a different color for each word, the patterns will be easier to see.

Words to Search For

Parallel
Parallel lines are always the same distance apart. They never meet or cross over each other.

Right Angle
A 90° angle, like the corner of a book, or the capital letter L.

Perpendicular
Straight up and down; at right angles to the surface (a telephone pole is usually perpendicular to the road).

Congruent
Exactly equal in shape and area.

Line
The path made by a moving point, sometimes straight, sometimes curved.

Rays
A group of lines coming from a center.

Bisect
To part into equal halves.

Rectangle
A figure with four sides that has four right angles.

```
V W M O B V H J K C W F I H F
A T H G I R O P G R U M L O C
N W M V S F J E N H E Z E H M
G J V / / / V R O H N C N F O
L F K Z E H O P C — T F I P L
E O W M C F W E M V J O L A E
C H J K T O V N F R E C E R L
S O C S J H S D V L E T N A L
J Y K Y L Y K I O G N A I L A
M J A A A Z M C J K O H L L R
S Y A R A Y S U G R U K E E A
O C A A A K J L N H E O N L P
F Y J Y H Y K A O H N F I O C
S O F S O J S R C — T V L M O
V P E R P E N D I C U L A R J
```

Paper Folding

Origami is the art of folding paper. You can make lots of intricate figures with origami; in fact, you may have seen an origami crane—one of the most popular origami animals.

The paper cranes are so well known because of Sadako, a Japanese girl who was dying of leukemia. Sadako heard an old legend: If a sick person folds one thousand origami cranes, the gods will grant her wish and make her healthy again. And so, she set out on a quest to fold one thousand cranes. Unfortunately, Sadako died before completing her project. Ever since then, people have been making origami cranes in memory of this bright girl.

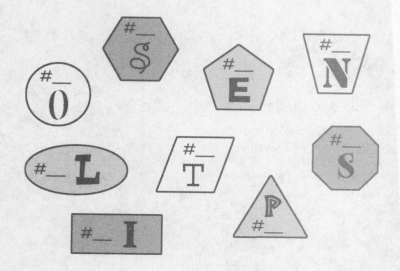

Sadako and Her Paper Cranes

Learn how to make paper cranes in memory of Sadako. Visit *www.personal. umich.edu/~adysart/origami/crane/* to learn how to make these paper creatures.

Life of the Party

Match each name to its geometric shape, numbering each shape as you go. Then, take the letter in each shape and place it in the corresponding box to get an old saying.

1. Triangle
2. Circle
3. Rectangle
4. Trapezoid
5. Rhombus
6. Ellipse
7. Pentagon
8. Hexagon
9. Octagon

Without geometry, life would be:

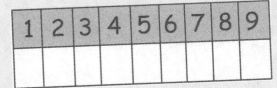

1	2	3	4	5	6	7	8	9

CIRCULAR REASONING

You have already learned something about circles in Chapter 1. Circles are certainly mysterious. The center of the circle is exactly the same distance to any point on the circle; that distance is known as the **radius.** Because circles cannot be measured by a ruler, you can't really divide them into inches or feet—but we can divide them into degrees.

A circle by any other name is just as round!

Compasses travel in the best circles!

Ho Ho Ho

Going Around in Circles

Find your way around the circles from start to end.

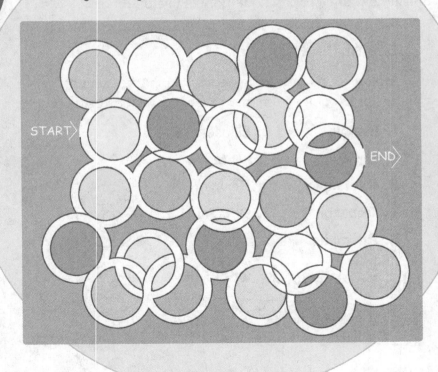

START>

END>

FUN FACT

360 Circles

A circle is divided into 360 degrees. But did you know that a golf ball has 360 dimples? Coincidence? We think not!

HEE HEE HEE

The Möbius Strip

Who knew that a simple strip of paper would be the subject of a puzzle problem, and that a man named Möbius would be forever remembered for it? Here is how a Möbius strip works.

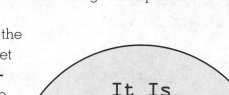

1. Take a long strip of paper—you can make one by cutting a piece of paper in several parts and taping them together to make one long strip.
2. Draw a circle on the top of the left end and one on top of the right end.
3. With one end in each hand, twist the paper once and then bring the two ends together and tape them together with the circles touching. This special loop is called a **Möbius strip.**
4. Now, take a black crayon and draw a line down the middle of the paper strip; keep going until you get back to where you started. **Here is your first surprise:** Your pen mark went from the outside to the inside and back. If you drove a miniature car over your strip, you would race over the "top" and "bottom" and find the start line and the finish line are the same place.
5. Now, take a pair of scissors and cut along the line you drew. You might think you would get two separate rings, just as you would when you cut a normal ring of paper. **Here is your second surprise:** You get one really big loop with several twists in it. For the **third surprise,** cut this long loop in half again.

It Is Mind-Boggling!

For an out-of-this-world experience, play tic-tac-toe on the surface of a torus or a klein bottle instead of a flat piece of paper at *www.northnet.org/weeks*. The maze is also a lot of fun, but the chess game is for expert players only.

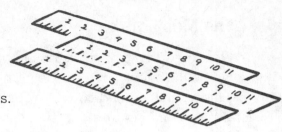

TAMPERING WITH TRIANGLES

What could be simpler than a triangle? It's a shape with three interconnected sides of any length. But actually, there are all kinds of triangles. Triangles may vary by the **length of their sides:**

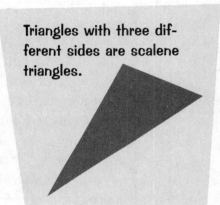

Triangles with three sides of equal length are equilateral triangles.

Triangles with two sides of equal length are isosceles triangles.

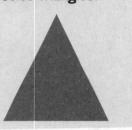

Triangles with three different sides are scalene triangles.

But that's not all! Triangles can also be sorted by their **angles:**

A triangle is equiangular (and, therefore, equilateral) if all its angles are congruent (same).

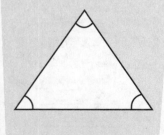

A triangle is a right triangle if one of its angles measures 90 degrees (and two of its sides are perpendicular to each other).

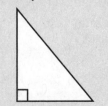

A triangle is obtuse if one of its angles is larger than 90 degrees.

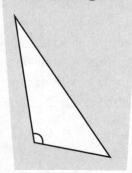

A triangle is acute if all three of its angles are smaller than 90 degrees.

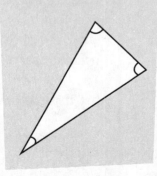

Triangle Numbers

Triangular numbers are found in the number of dots that can be used to make an equilateral triangle (triangle with three equal sides). The following illustrations represent 3, 6, 10, and 15.
Can you see a pattern here?

$$1 + 2 = 3 \qquad 1 + 2 + 3 = 6 \qquad 1 + 2 + 3 + 4 = 10 \qquad 1 + 2 + 3 + 4 + 5 = 15$$

Draw a picture or add numbers to find the next three triangular numbers.

The next three numbers are 21, 28, and 36.

The only angle from which to approach a problem is the try-angle!

Ho Ho Ho

The Last Straw

If you take three drinking straws, you can easily arrange them into one triangle that has three equal sides. Now, suppose you have six drinking straws. Can you arrange them into FOUR triangles, all with equal sides?

HINT: You may need some tape!

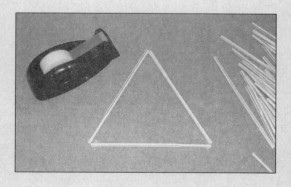

Get to the Point!

Color every triangle in this puzzle to find the answer to the following riddle:

If you have ten cats in a box and one jumps out, how many are left?

NONE — THEY'RE ALL COPY CATS!

Magic Pentagrams

This puzzle is just for fun—there's no right or wrong answer!

Choose a number found on one of the points of a pentagram. Now, point to all the pentagrams on which this number can be found. Add the large number found in the center of those pentagrams. The sum will be the number that you chose!

Share the magic pentagram trick with a friend, or try making your own pentagram puzzle using different numbers.

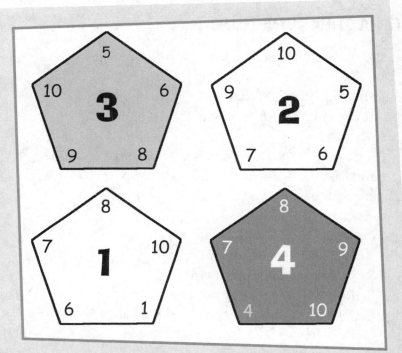

FUN FACT

Gargantuan Geometry

Did you know that one of the largest pentagons in the world is right here in the United States? That's right—the Pentagon building just outside Washington, D.C., which serves as the headquarters of the Department of Defense, is so big that the National Capitol could fit into any one of its five wedge-shaped sections. To get around inside, there are 17.5 miles of corridors! Want to know more fascinating facts about this prominent polygon? Check out *www.fortamerica.com/about-the-pentagon.html*.

SpiroGraphs

Create your own SpiroGraph design at *www.math.ucsd.edu/~dlittle/java/SpiroGraph.html*. There are suggestions for the different settings; try them all. Make the String of Pearls for someone special.

ON A TREASURE HUNT

The not-so-famous outlaw Cash Steele hid all the money he stole somewhere in or near the town of Nowhere, Nevada. After he died, his daughter, Penny, went looking for the treasure.

She knew her father very well. After looking around town, she decided that there were ten possible places where he could have hidden his money:

1. Under the dirt floor of his cabin.
2. In the hayloft of his barn.
3. In the Steele family cemetery.
4. High up in the branches of the Lone Pine Tree.
5. On top of Windy Hill.
6. In the cave to the east of Windy Hill.
7. In the old mine shaft.
8. At the top of the windmill.
9. In a pile of dinosaur bones.
10. Down at the bottom of the well.

Here is what else Penny knew:

1. Her father was afraid of ghosts and wouldn't want his money close to the cemetery.
2. Cash Steele did not like small dark places either.
3. If he buried the money, it would be to the north of his cabin.
4. If he hid it aboveground, it would be south of the cabin.
5. If he didn't hide it in the well, then he didn't hide it in the windmill, either.

That leaves one possible hiding place. What is it?

(See the answer on page 129 for an explanation.)

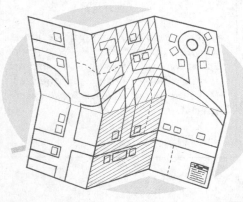

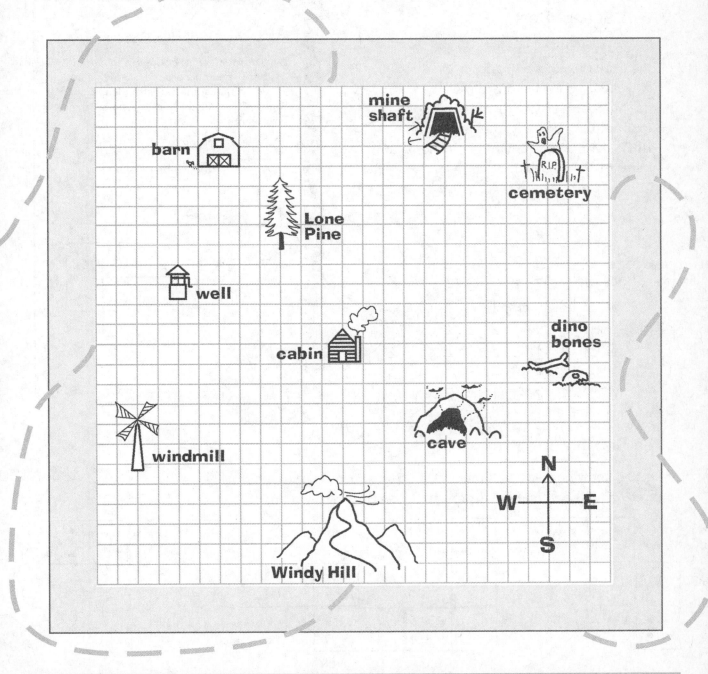

A Square Deal

Begin at the white number 4 that is in the dark box. Move up, down, or sideways four spaces in any direction. Add the numbers as you go and reach all four corners, but only one time each. **HINT: the pattern forms the outline of a letter of the alphabet.**

```
4 2 4 3 1 3 4 2 4
2 1 2 4 3 4 2 1 2
1 2 4 3 2 3 4 2 3
3 4 3 2 1 2 3 4 1
4 3 2 1 4 1 2 1 2
3 4 3 2 1 2 3 4 1
1 2 4 3 2 3 4 2 3
2 1 2 4 1 4 2 1 2
4 2 4 1 3 1 4 2 4
```

Depth of the Matter

What's the difference between a square and a cube? The number of dimensions. Squares are **two-dimensional** (they have length and width). Cubes are **three-dimensional** (they have length, width, and depth).

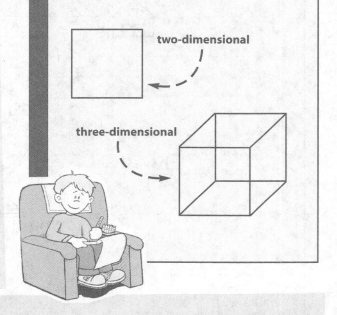

two-dimensional

three-dimensional

The Domino Effect

Do you know how to play dominoes? See if you can figure it out by filling in the missing squares. HINT: Each number, from 1 to 6, can only be used once.

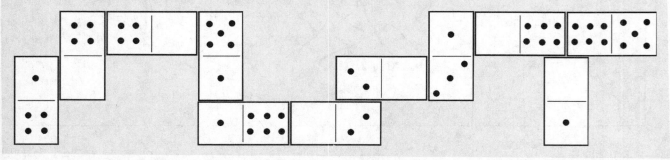

Picture This

Look at the patterns below. Try to picture which shapes can be folded into a square box that has four sides, a top, and a bottom. Circle the correct answers. HINT: Having trouble picturing this in your mind? Use a ruler and a pen to draw the shapes onto heavy paper, cut them out, and see which shapes will actually fold into a box.

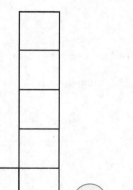

①

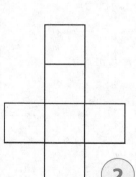
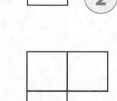

② ③

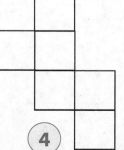
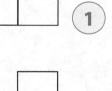

④

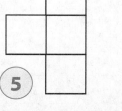

⑤ ⑥

Box 1
Yes ☐
No ☐

Box 2
Yes ☐
No ☐

Box 3
Yes ☐
No ☐

Box 4
Yes ☐
No ☐

Box 5
Yes ☐
No ☐

Box 6
Yes ☐
No ☐

NOTES

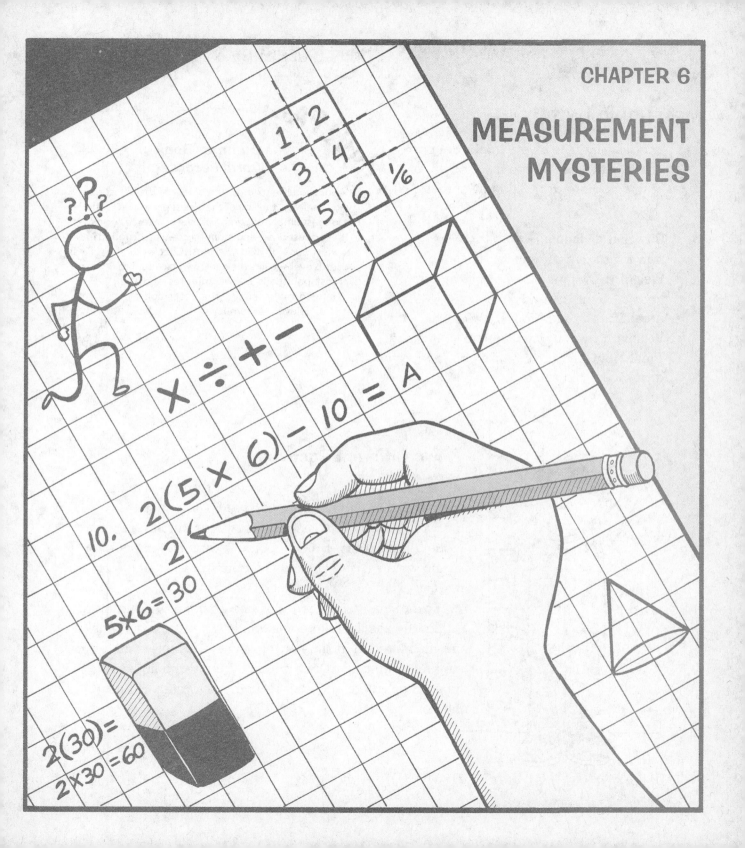

CHAPTER 6

MEASUREMENT MYSTERIES

MEASURING UNITS

Measurement is a very important part of everyday life. We measure all sorts of things. Here are just a few of them:

- **Size and distance:** How tall you are; how far away your school is.
- **Weight:** How much do you weigh; how heavy is your backpack.
- **Area:** How large is your apartment.
- **Volume:** How much water is in your bathtub.
- **Time:** How long does it take you to read this paragraph; how old you are.

FUN FACT

The Guinness Book of World Records

Would you like to know the height of the tallest man who ever lived, the age of the oldest person on Earth, or the longest time spent riding a roller coaster? The answers to these questions—and *many* more—can be found in *The Guinness Book of World Records*! Check out the silliest records ever set, like the person who caught the most paintballs in two minutes and the person who kissed the most cobras (eleven of them!).

HEE
HEE
HEE

Two Different Systems

There are two main systems of measurement in the world today. In America, we use the **English system,** which involves units such as inches, feet, yards, and miles for measuring lengths; ounces, pounds, and tons for measuring weights; and cups, pints, quarts, and gallons for measuring liquid volumes.

Most of the rest of the world (including, more and more, England) uses the **metric system.** In this system, lengths are measured in millimeters, centimeters, meters, and kilometers; weights in grams and kilograms; and liquid volumes in milliliters and liters. The metric system is based on the base of 10.

A Metric Mnemonic

A **mnemonic** is a memory trick to help you remember tricky information. The metric system is based on factors of 10, but the words used to represent each multiplication (or division) by 10 are easy to confuse. Here is a mnemonic device to remember the order of the prefixes in the metric system.

Kilo ↔ **H**ecto ↔ **D**eka ↔ unit ↔ **D**eci ↔ **C**enti ↔ **M**illi

Each arrow represents a factor of 10. When you move to the right, the measure gets smaller (divide by 10) for each arrow. When you move to the left, the measure gets larger (multiply by 10).

WORDS 2 KNOW

metric prefixes: A prefix is a part of the word that is added on at the beginning of the root. The following prefixes are added to "meter," "gram," and "liter" to form metric measurements:

> **Milli–** 1/1,000
> **Centi–** 1/100
> **Deci–** 1/10
> **Deka–** 10
> **Hecto–** 100
> **Kilo–** 1,000

☞ **Here's a story to help you remember the order of the names of the prefixes:**

During medieval times, <u>K</u>ings considered themselves to be above all other <u>H</u>umans, and Humans considered themselves to be above the <u>D</u>ragons. These are the mighty and all are above the basic unit. Below the basic unit are <u>D</u>ogs, which considered themselves to be above <u>C</u>ats, which considered themselves to be above <u>M</u>ice.

"Three Blind Mice" in Metrics

You can sing the metric hierarchy to the beginning of the tune of "Three Blind Mice": **K**ings, **H**umans, **D**ragons, **D**ogs, **C**ats, **M**ice.

Convenient OR *Confusing?*

Many people believe that the English system is needlessly confusing because it's hard to convert from one measurement to another, and that we should switch to the metric system. But others believe that because we have grown up with the English system, we should continue using it because it's easier than learning a new one. **Which group do you agree with?**

NOT BY A LONG SHOT

How do we measure length and distance? With inches, feet, yards, miles—or with millimeters, centimeters, meters, and kilometers. Here is the conversion table:

1 mile = 5,280 feet 1 yard = 3 feet 1 foot = 12 inches	1 kilometer = 1,000 meters 1 meter = 100 centimeters 1 centimeter = 10 millimeters
1 mile = 1.61 kilometers 1 foot = 0.3048 meters 1 inch = 2.54 centimeters	1 kilometer = 0.6214 miles 1 meter = 39.37 inches 1 millimeter = 0.0394 inches

Q: Why did the metric chicken cross the road?

A: To see how many meters wide it was.

Answer the following questions and then fill in the answer key to find out which animal's tongue can grow up to 21 inches long—about as long as your arm. Slurp!

1. How long is a school bus?

   f) 6 feet
   g) 36 feet
   h) 160 feet
   i) 6 yards

2. How long is a twin bed?

   h) 6 inches
   i) 6 feet
   j) 60 inches
   k) 60 feet

3. How long is a football field?

   r) 360 feet
   s) 360 inches
   t) 36 miles
   u) 360 miles

4. How long is a dollar bill?

   a) 6 inches
   b) 60 centimeters
   c) 6 feet
   d) 6 millimeters

5. How long is a marathon?

   c) 26.2 meters
   d) 262 centimeters
   e) 262 kilometers
   f) 26.2 miles

6. How long is a blue whale?

   c) 10 meters
   d) 100 inches
   e) 100 feet
   f) 10 yards

1	2	3	4	5	5	6

Hink Pinks

Each silly answer in the following Hink Pinks is made up of two words that rhyme. HINT: The first six are one-syllable words; the last Hink Pink is made up of words that are two syllables each.

1. Pile of games that weighs 2,000 lbs. _____

2. 5,280 foot grin _____

3. Two pastries that are each 12 inches long _____

4. Very difficult 3 feet _____

5. Rubber ball that weighs 16 ounces _____

6. 28.4 grams that jumps quickly _____

7. Urgent message that weighs 2.2 pounds _____

To St. Ives

As I was going to St. Ives
I met a man with seven wives.
Each wife had six sacks,
Each sack had five cats,
Each cat had four kits,
Each kit had three mice,
Each mouse had two pieces of cheese,
Each cheese had one toothpick.

How many toothpicks were there?

Math Online

Journey across 42 powers of 10 at *www.wordwizz.com/pwrsof10.htm*. These pictures show one image at the submolecular level enlarged to 10 times as big, over and over until you are looking at the entire known universe. Choose the smallest image and then keep clicking on the +1 button to increase the zoom by a factor of 10.

Chapter   1   2   3   4   5

Star Power

Find the perfect center of this starry pattern.

START

FINISH

A WEIGHTY MATTER

It helps to know how much things weigh. We measure candy in ounces, fruit and vegetables in pounds, and elephants in tons. Here are the conversion tables for metric and English weight measurements.

1 ton = 2,000 pounds 1 pound = 16 ounces	1 kilogram = 1,000 grams 1 gram = 1,000 milligrams
1 ton = 1,016.05 kilograms 1 pound = 0.45 kilograms 1 ounce = 28.4 grams	1 kilogram = 2.2 pounds 1 gram = 0.035 ounces

I am the world's largest animal. I can weigh 177 tons—that's 354,000 pounds. It would take more than 4,400 children averaging 80 pounds each to balance with me!

1. How much does an average man weigh?	2. How much did a Tyrannosaurus rex weigh?
a) 172 ounces b) 172 pounds c) 172 grams d) 172 kilograms	j) 60 kilograms k) 60 pounds l) 6 tons m) 60 tons

continued on facing page

Chapter 1 2 3 4 5

continued from previous page

3. How much does an adult polar bear weigh?

u) 1,400 pounds
v) 140 pounds
w) 14 kilograms
x) 140 tons

6. How much does an ant weigh?

h) 4 milligrams
i) 4 kilograms
j) 4 ounces
k) 4 pounds

4. How much does this book weigh?

c) 11 grams
d) 11 milligrams
e) 11 ounces
f) 11 pounds

7. How much does an apple weigh?

a) 160 grams
b) 160 ounces
c) 16 pounds
d) 16 grams

5. How much does a nickel weigh?

w) 5 grams
x) 0.05 ounces
y) 50 ounces
z) 50 grams

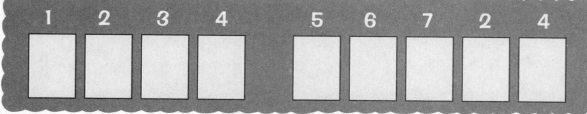

1	2	3	4	5	6	7	2	4

Chapter 6   7   8   9   Appendix

Measuring Your ZZZs

Write each letter in the space above the measurement that matches its place on the ruler. When you're finished, you will have the answer to the following riddle:

Why did the math teacher take a nap with a ruler?

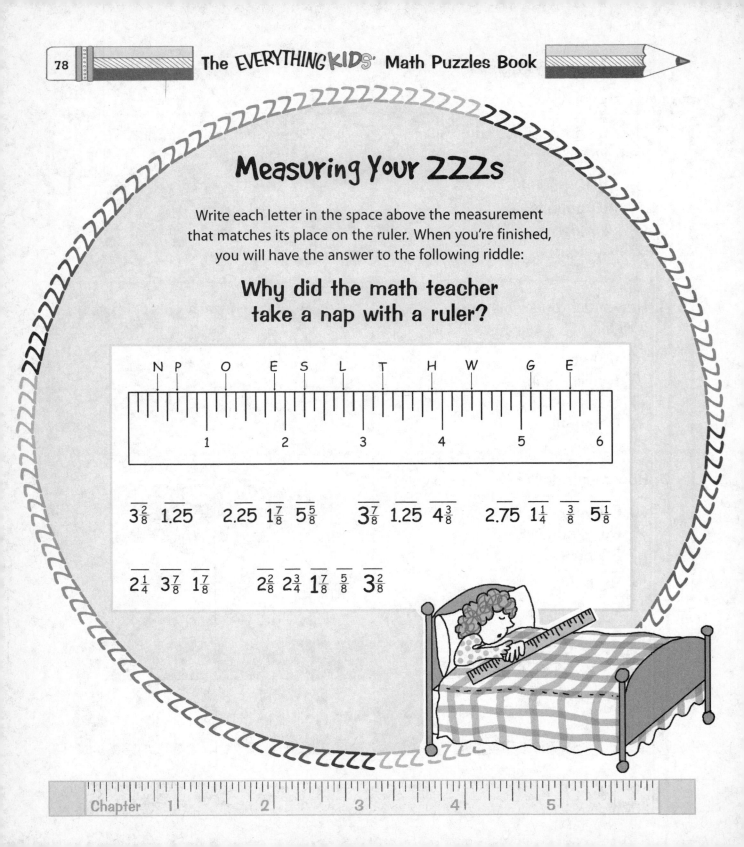

$$3\tfrac{2}{8}\ \overline{}\ 1.25\ \overline{}\quad 2.25\ \overline{}\ 1\tfrac{7}{8}\ \overline{}\ 5\tfrac{5}{8}\ \overline{}\quad 3\tfrac{7}{8}\ \overline{}\ 1.25\ \overline{}\ 4\tfrac{3}{8}\ \overline{}\quad 2.75\ \overline{}\ 1\tfrac{1}{4}\ \overline{}\ \tfrac{3}{8}\ \overline{}\ 5\tfrac{1}{8}\ \overline{}$$

$$2\tfrac{1}{4}\ \overline{}\ 3\tfrac{7}{8}\ \overline{}\ 1\tfrac{7}{8}\ \overline{}\quad 2\tfrac{2}{8}\ \overline{}\ 2\tfrac{3}{4}\ \overline{}\ 1\tfrac{7}{8}\ \overline{}\ \tfrac{5}{8}\ \overline{}\ 3\tfrac{2}{8}\ \overline{}$$

STACKING UP ZEROS

Why is the metric system based on 10? Because our entire number system is built on multiples of 10. Think of it this way: You've got 1, 2, 3, 4, 5, 6, 7, 8, 9, and then you go back to 1 and just add a 0 to it—10. Add another 0, and you get 100. How many zeros can you keep on stacking? Take a look here:

NUMBER OF ZEROS	WHAT YOU GET
0	one
1	ten
2	hundred
3	thousand
4	ten thousand
5	hundred thousand
6	million
7	ten million
8	hundred million
9	billion
12	trillion
16	quadrillion
100	googol
googol	googolplex

Lost Billions

It looks like there are billions and billions of the word **BILLIONS** in this grid, but it only appears correctly spelled one time. It could be left to right, up and down, diagonal, or even backward.

```
B I L L I O N N S B B I
B I L S B S N O I L I B
I B S S N B I L L O N S
L S N N B O B I L L N O
L N I O I I B B O B I
L O O I L B O L I B I L
I I L L O B S I L O B I
O L L L O N L B O I S L
N L I B I L I O B B I I
S I B L I B O B I L I B
I B L B B I L O O N S I
O B B I L I O O N S O L
```

Googols of Fun

A googol is a **REALLY** big number. If a ten has one zero (10), how many zeros do you think a googol has? Using a simple number substitution (A=1, B=2, C=3, etc.), see if you can break this number code.

1   7·15·15·7·15·12   8·1·19

__   __ __ __ __ __ __   __ __ __

15·14·5   8·21·14·4·18·5·4

__ __ __   __ __ __ __ __ __ __

26·5·18·15·19

__ __ __ __ __

What's Beyond Googolplex?

The rules of math say that you can keep counting for infinity. That means, numbers keep going and going, and there is no such thing as the last or highest number. Infinity is not a number—it's a concept that something is never-ending. Mathematicians use ∞ to represent infinity in mathematical calculations.

Counting Forever

The symbol ∞ has been around for more than two thousand years. The Romans used it to represent 1,000, a BIG number to them. Around the year 1650, an English mathematician, John Wallis, proposed that this symbol ∞ be used to represent infinity, and we have been doing just that ever since.

On Your Toes

Use this fraction code to figure out the riddle.

CODE

The white part of each shape is empty. The shaded part of each shape is filled. Estimate how much of each shape is full using the following rules:

If the shape is almost empty, call it 0.
If the shape is almost full, call it 1.
If the shape is between full and empty, call it ½.

HOW TO USE THE CODE

Look at the fraction or number below each blank. Using the shapes connected to each word box, pick the shape that is closest to that fraction or number. Write the letter of that shape on the blank.

RIDDLE: How does a math student make her shoes longer?

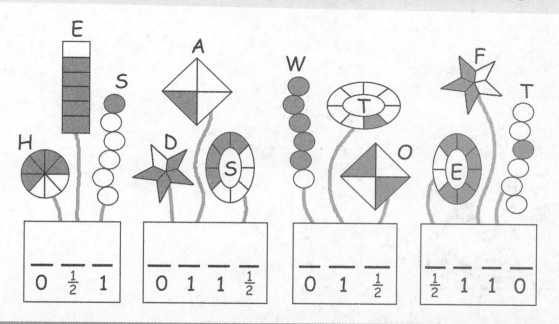

NOTES

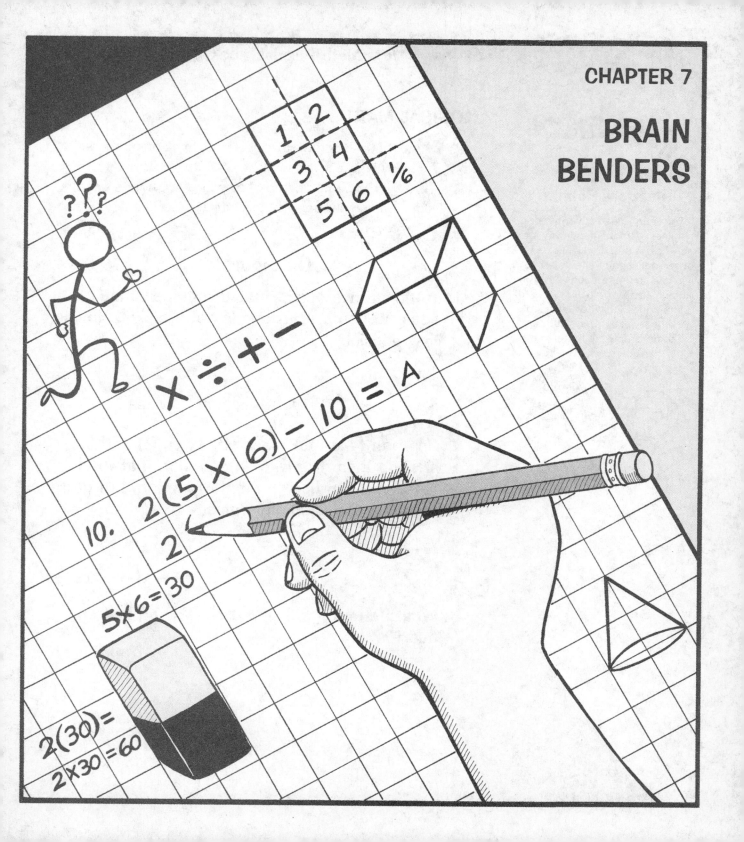

CHAPTER 7

BRAIN BENDERS

FUN FACT

Just Like Sherlock Holmes

The fictional detective Sherlock Holmes is famous for using logic to solve cases based on clues he had observed. Logic and reasoning allow us to figure things out using known facts or clues instead of simply guessing. All of us use logic every day of our lives, although some people are better at it than others.

LOGICAL MATH

Most of us, when we think of math, think of numbers. But not all math involves numbers. You've already explored some geometry activities in Chapter 5 that involved lines and shapes. Another area of math that does not have to involve numbers is logic.

Go Figure!

1. You have two coins. Added together, they equal 15 cents—but one is not a nickel. How is that possible?

2. Can you take four nines (9, 9, 9, 9) and arrange them to make an equation that totals 100? You can use any math function, but you can only use each nine once.

3. What do you get if you divide 30 by half and add 10?

4. If there are five apples and you take away three, how many apples do you have?

....

....

5. What is the meaning of FaπCE?

....

....

6. What is the meaning of MILONELION?

....

....

7. What is the meaning of this phrase: ONE, ONE, ONE, ONE, ONE, ONE, ANOTHER, ANOTHER, ANOTHER, ANOTHER, ANOTHER, ANOTHER?

....

....

8. A clerk in a butcher shop is 6' 2" tall. What does he weigh?

....

....

Moving Around

See if you can use logic to solve the puzzle about four fast friends: Gary, Harry, Larry, and Mary who lived in Los Angeles. One day, the four friends got news that they would be moving to four different cities: Atlanta, Boston, Chicago, and Dallas. By listening to their parents talk, the friends learned the following:

✱ Gary's family was moving to either Boston or Dallas.

✱ Harry's family was not moving to either Boston or Chicago.

✱ Either Harry or Mary was moving to Atlanta.

✱ If Harry moves to Atlanta, then Gary moves to Chicago.

✱ If Larry moves to Chicago, then Gary does not move to Dallas.

Who is moving where? Use the table to figure out the answer.

	ATLANTA	BOSTON	CHICAGO	DALLAS
Gary				
Harry				
Larry				
Mary				

IN THE ENCHANTED KINGDOM

The logic puzzles on this page take place in an enchanted kingdom, at a castle inhabited by four princesses—Ruby, Sapphire, Jade, and Topaz—as well as their mother, Queen Diamond, and their four pet dragons.

Taming Dragons

These princesses don't need anyone to rescue them—they are dragon tamers and have four days to tame their four dragons. Every day, each one must work with a different dragon. On the **second day**, Ruby tamed Spitfire and Sapphire tamed Forktail. On the **third day,** Jade tamed Blaze and Topaz tamed Smokey. On the **fourth day,** Sapphire tamed Smokey and Topaz tamed Forktail. **Which dragon did each princess tame on each day?**

	DAY 1	DAY 2	DAY 3	DAY 4
Ruby				
Jade				
Sapphire				
Topaz				

The Marriage Proposal

Prince Pyrite came to the enchanted castle to ask for Princess Ruby's hand in marriage, but Ruby didn't like him. The Queen didn't want to offend Prince Pyrite, who was her guest, so she told him to go to her garden and put one black and one white pebble into his purse. If Ruby picks a **black** pebble, they will marry. If she picks a **white** one, the prince will have to go home alone.

As the prince went out to the garden, Ruby followed him and saw him put two black pebbles into the purse. At first, she's dismayed but then gets an idea. **How can Ruby trick the prince?**

IN THE LAND OF CONFUSION

All the people in the Land of Confusion are either sages or jesters. **Sages** are noted for their honesty—they always tell the truth. **Jesters,** however, are always kidding around and never tell the truth. Unfortunately, there is no way to tell one from the other just by looking at them.

Ima Visitor leaves her home in the Enchanted Kingdom and travels to the Land of Confusion. While there, she meets three men: Xavier, Yale, and Zachary. Ima asks, "How many of you are sages?"

Xavier says that he is not a jester.
Yale says that Xavier is lying.
Zachary adds, "Yale is lying."

Can you figure out who is a sage and who is a jester?

Two Kids in the Land of Confusion

Ima keeps on walking. Just as she approaches the emperor's palace, she finds a boy and a girl sitting on the steps, and hears three statements:

1. "I'm a boy," says the child with black hair.
2. "I'm a girl," says the child with red hair.
3. "Exactly one of us is a sage," says the boy.

Are the boy and girl sages and/or jesters, and what color hair does each one have?

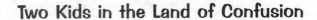

A Boast?

Upon entering the emperor's palace, Ima overheard a man say, "If I am a sage, then so is my son."

What can you tell about him or his son?

You will find the answers in the Puzzle Answers section, page 131.

Meeting the King

Inside the palace, Ima went looking for the King, and she met some sages. She asked them if the King is a sage or a jester, and they told her that they didn't know, but that according to their laws, he must be a citizen of the Land of Confusion, either a sage or a jester.

Just then, a man entered the hall wearing a crown and a beautiful purple cloak. The sages told Ima that it was the King, and that she could ask him whether he was a sage or a jester. To her question, the King responded, "I am a jester."

Immediately, the sages cried: "Imposter! Arrest that man!" Why?

Einstein's Math Troubles

"Do not worry too much about your difficulties in mathematics, I can assure you mine are still greater."

—Albert Einstein

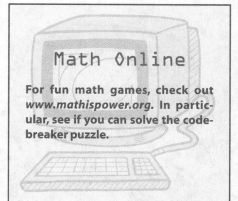

Math Online

For fun math games, check out *www.mathispower.org*. In particular, see if you can solve the code-breaker puzzle.

Chapter 6 7 8 9 Appendix

Read the Numbers

Numbers are used for counting, but did you know they can also be used for spelling? Numbers like 4, 8, and 2 sound the same as familiar words we use all the time. People who want to write short messages often substitute a single number for a group of letters. For example, "L8" spells "late" but uses only two characters instead of four. This kind of number spelling is often used on license plates, where there is room for only six or seven characters. **See if you can match the following people with their fancy license plates:**

1. Musician who plays a big horn.

2. A person who is always lucky.

3. Someone who is very polite.

4. A person who is always happy.

5. Someone who can predict the weather.

6. A person who is hardly ever on time.

7. ~~Artist.~~

8. Someone who is impatient.

9. A person with a bad memory.

10. Someone who likes surprises.

11. A frequent visitor to a skating rink.

12. Someone who likes a particular sport.

CR8TV

1DRFL

42N8

7. CREATIVE

4EVRL8

I4GOT

10SNY1

H82W8

2BA

W8NC

4CAST

10Q

SK8R

Simple Symbols

Each symbol below equals one of the possible numbers in the box. Substitute the numbers for the symbols so that the subtraction problems work.

HINT: All numbers in the top row are greater than or equal to their corresponding place numbers in the bottom row. We have also left you two zeros to get you started.

Possible numbers: 1 2 4 6

✂ ⊙ ✌   ⊙ ✌ ✂
− ☆ ✌ ✌   − ✌ ✌ ⊙
⊙ ✌ 0   ✌ 0 ☆

Q: Where's the best place to hide if you're scared?

A: Inside a math book—because there's safety in numbers.

A Card Game

Two kids play five games of gin rummy. Each kid wins the same number of games, but there are no tied games. How is this possible?

The two kids weren't playing each other!

Buying Numbers

This conversation doesn't add up. Can you tell what's for sale?

Customer: How much is 1?

Salesman: 30 cents.

Customer: I'd like 14, please.

Salesman: That will be 60 cents.

Customer: Oops, I really need 114.

Salesman: No problem. That will be 90 cents.

$$\begin{array}{ccccccccc} 1 & 2 & 2 & 1 & 3 & 1 & 2 & 3 & 5 \\ 2 & 2 & 3 & 3 & 1 & 2 & 1 & 4 & 1 \\ 1 & 2 & 1 & 2 & 5 & 2 & 2 & 1 & 2 \\ 2 & 3 & 1 & 4 & 3 & 1 & 4 & 2 & 5 \\ 1 & 2 & 3 & 4 & 2 & 3 & 3 & 4 & 4 \\ 4 & 1 & 5 & 2 & 1 & 2 & 1 & 3 & 3 \\ 5 & 3 & 4 & 1 & 2 & 4 & 4 & 5 & 5 \\ 1 & 2 & 2 & 1 & 3 & 4 & 5 & 1 & 2 \\ 3 & 1 & 1 & 2 & 4 & 3 & 3 & 2 & 1 \end{array}$$

I Can't Find It!

The numbers 1, 2, 3, 4, and 5 appear in a row only one time in this number grid! The answer can be up, down, side to side, or diagonal. Look extra carefully—the numbers might also appear backward!

Math Puzzles

I Found It!

Mr. Math asked four of his students to see how many math puzzle books they could find in the public library. How many books did each student find? Use the clues to complete the chart.

Students	# of books each student found
Jasmine	
Katlyn	
Josh	
Ethan	
TOTAL number of puzzle books found	

1. The four students found a total of 13 math puzzle books.
2. None of the students found more than 5 puzzle books.
3. None of the children found the same number of puzzle books.
4. Jasmine found 3 puzzle books.
5. Katlyn found fewer puzzle books than Jasmine.
6. Ethan found the most puzzle books.

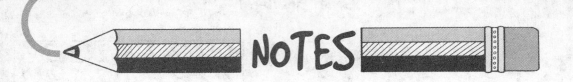

NOTES

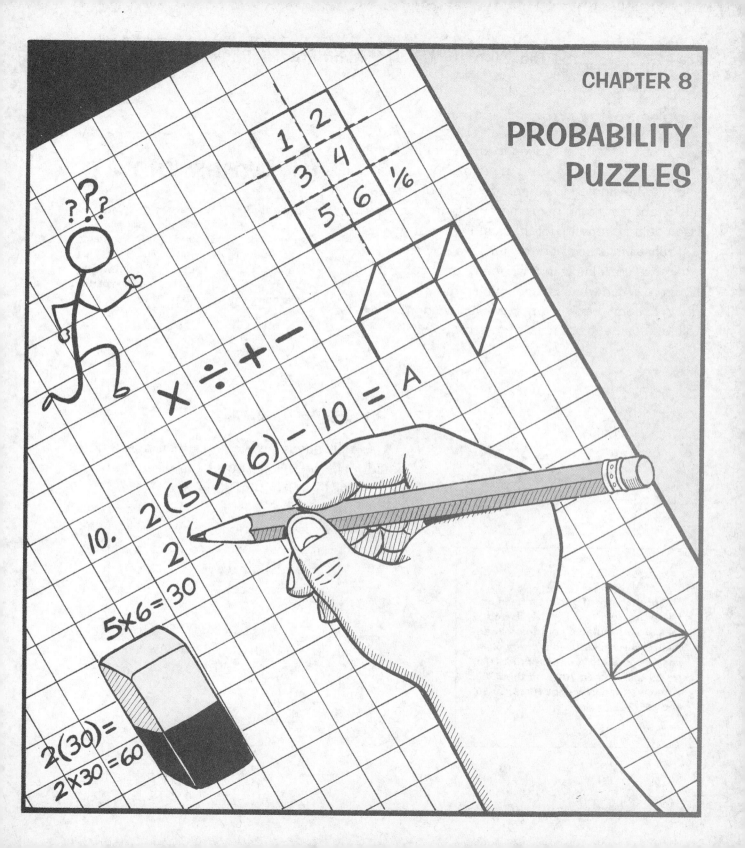

A PROBABLE CAUSE

You might be surprised to know that probability is a relatively new area of math. Probability began to be studied in the mid-1600s. That may seem like a long time ago, but remember that people have been doing geometry for thousands of years.

Probability is involved any time we do something where we can't know in advance what is going to happen. When we toss a coin in the air, we know it is going to come back down. However, we don't know if it will land as heads or tails. That is probability.

WORDS 2 KNOW

probability: The chances of something happening—actually, the ratio of the number of times it could happen compared to the number of possible things that could happen. For example, when you throw dice, you have 1/6 chances of getting each particular number.

Probability Scrabble

Can you guess how many other words you could make by using any of the eleven letters in the word PROBABILITY? Do you think you could make fifty words, or is the number closer to twenty? There is no way to know except by sitting down with paper and pencil and making a list.

For each word, you can use each letter as many times as it appears in PROBABILITY. For example, you could spell BABY because there are two Bs, but you can't spell ROOT, because there is only one O.

A Coin Toss

The probability of getting a head or a tail in any coin toss is ½ heads and ½ tails. Do a simulated coin-toss experiment at www.acs.ilstu.edu/faculty/bllim/java/progsinnotes/CoinToss.html. First, try 25 tosses, then 100, and then 500. When we tried it, we got 10/15, 50/50, and 251/249.

PLAYING DICE

When you roll the die, you are playing with probability. With each roll, you are just as likely to get 1 as you are 2, 3, 4, 5, or 6. That means that you have one in six chances to get any number. And each time you throw the die, the probability of getting a particular number remains the same.

What If You Roll Two Dice?

Can you figure out what your probabilities are of getting a 1, 2, 3, 4, 5, or 6 if you roll two dice? Will your chances increase or decrease?

Your chances will increase to 2/6 or 1/3.

Prisoners Game

This is a game for two players. To play, you will need the following:

- **Five pennies and five nickels (or two sets of other markers)**
- **A pair of dice**
- **Paper and pencil for keeping score**

Players should each have five markers, which are prisoners. Player 1 places his or her five prisoners in each cell of the top row. Player 2 places prisoners in the bottom row. Players take turns rolling the dice and subtracting the smaller number from the larger. If the difference matches a cell number, the prisoner kept in that cell goes free (is taken off the board). **Whoever frees all the prisoners first, wins!**

A Variation on the Prisoners Game

This time, each player picks where to put his or her prisoners. For example, Player 1 could put a prisoner in cells 1, 2, and 3 of the top row and cells 3, 4, and 5 of the bottom row. Each roll of the dice frees two prisoners at a time. After playing several rounds, who has the best strategy?

Who Owns That Car?

A man came in to the motor vehicle department to register his new car. He requested a very special license plate with the numbers 337 31770. While signing the paperwork, the mysterious man said, "Now everyone will know that this car belongs to me!" **What was the man's name?**

337 31770

Let 'er Roll!

Unlike the Prisoners Game, this one offers equal chances of winning to all the players, and you can have as many as six people join the game. Here is what you will need to play:

- **Piece of paper and pencil for each player**
- **Pair of dice**

You also need to make a game card for each player. To do that, draw a five-squares-by-five-squares grid—you can use a ruler to make the lines straight, but it doesn't matter if they're wobbly.

Then, have one player read the following list of numbers:

1, 36, 9, 24, 18, 8, 6, 15, 30, 25, 10, 24, 18, 6, 3, 12, 2, 4, 12, 16, 9, 12, 16, 9, 12, 20, 6, 10

As each number is called out, each player should write it down in any one of the squares in the grid, until all the spaces are filled. Some numbers will appear twice.

Once you are done, the game can begin. Players take turn rolling the two dice, multiplying the two results, and then covering one number on the grid. **The first one to cover five squares in a row (in any direction) is the winner.**

Even and Odd

Here is a game that uses a principle similar to the Prisoners Game and Let'er Roll. To play, you will need two players: **Player E** (even) and **Player O** (odd), plus the following:

- **Piece of paper**
- **Pencil**
- **Paper clip**

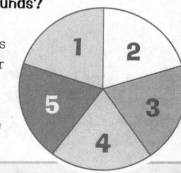

Let's see, 2 x 3 = 6. That's an even number, so I win!

On the count of three, both players show each other one to five fingers on one hand. Multiply the number of fingers showing on one player's hand by the number of fingers showing on the other player's hand. If the product is even, Player E wins. If the product is odd, Player O wins. Keep a tally for twenty rounds. **Which player wins the most rounds?**

You should have noticed that Player E won many more games than Player O. Will Player E still win if both players use a spinner instead of their fingers? Try it. Use a pencil to hold a paper clip at the center of the spinner. Flick the paper clip around the spinner. Keep a tally for twenty rounds. **Now, which player won the most games?**

Space
for
Tallies

(see the following page for possible explanations)

Even and Odd—Explained

What's going on? Why does Player E keep winning? There are two possible explanations:

1. If Player E always shows either two or four fingers, the answer will *always* be even, regardless of the number of fingers Player O shows. Player E will win *every time*.

2. If Player E is totally honest and shows fingers randomly, then it is the same as using the spinner. Player E will win most of the time. To see why, **fill in this multiplication table** and circle all the even numbers. Wow!

×	1	2	3	4	5
1	1	2	3		
2	2	4			
3	3				
4					
5					

▲ When you look at the results, it's easy to see which kind of number is more likely to win!

Get Out of Here

Make your way from START to END by following a number path that goes even, odd, even, odd, etc.

How many different paths do you think you might start before you find the correct one?

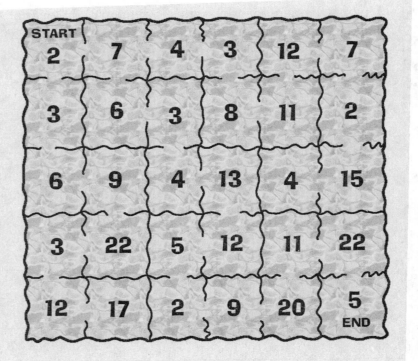

START
2	7	4	3	12	7
3	6	3	8	11	2
6	9	4	13	4	15
3	22	5	12	11	22
12	17	2	9	20	5 END

An Average Day

What do you know about estimating averages? Each blank below represents an average value. Fill in the following story with your estimates:

I'm just an average ten-year-old who is ⬭ inches tall. I am in school for ⬭ hours per year. After school, I eat a snack. Usually it's popcorn. One popped kernel weighs about ⬭ grams and there are about ⬭ popped kernels in one cup. Today, we are out of popcorn, so I eat ice cream. My favorite flavor is ⬭ . I watch a half-hour TV show, but there is an average of ⬭ commercials every 30 minutes, so the show is really only ⬭ minutes long. Before I go to bed, I still check under the bed for monsters. After all, there is an average of ⬭ monsters per bed.

▶ One of the averages above is a mode. Which one is it? _____

Q: What's an average pie?

A: Pie à la mode.

WORDS 2 KNOW

averages: There are three ways to calculate the average. The **mean** is what you get if you add up all the values and divide the total by the number of values. This is typically what people mean when they use the word **average**. The **median** of a set of values is the value in the middle of the set when the set is written in order. The **mode** of a set of values is the value that occurs most often. Mode is usually used as the average when the values are not numbers, like eye or hair color.

Hidden Numbers, Etc.

There are ten sentences hidden in this grid, and only one sentence per line, but here's the trick: Within each sentence are letters that spell out a number **ONE** through **TEN**. In the grid, though, the spelled-out numbers have been replaced by the corresponding

```
B U T T E R H Y T F L Y T O P 7 3 Y R E S
T H E 2 I O F 1 0 E A T H E R E W E 9 S H
B E P U T A P E 9 A C H B A G W H E T 2 M
W H E N I 8 A N Y T R E B M K 9 0 4 V A T
7 O U R W 8 H E A P P L E S P L E A S E 8
I T I 7 N O T O D D I F 1 C B 2 B N 3 M O
B O P N E S 5 9 Y S E E I 5 G O T M A I L
M Y C A T W H A T I 4 P H 1 R I N G S R I
W H Y 7 J I M L P O T T E R S R E W 5 D U
T T H E P O N D I S F I L L E D W I 3 D S
V I T A M I 4 T H A 2 U L D B E N I C E K
N Y T H R T H I S I S A 4 A S T Y J I O B
6 T H E S H E I S T O 1 A R T H E E D G E
H E H A S A B A R 9 A S T C O N C O R D H
B U T I 6 D O N 2 R R Y B E H A P P Y P Y
```

(continued)

digits 1 through 10. Circle the sentences as you find them and write them out with correct spelling, and don't forget the punctuation! **HINT:** The sentences are all horizontal, but not every line has a hidden sentence in it.

SAMPLE: _____ I often eat here. _____

1. _____

2. _____

3. _____

4. _____

5. _____

6. _____

7. _____

8. _____

9. _____

10. _____

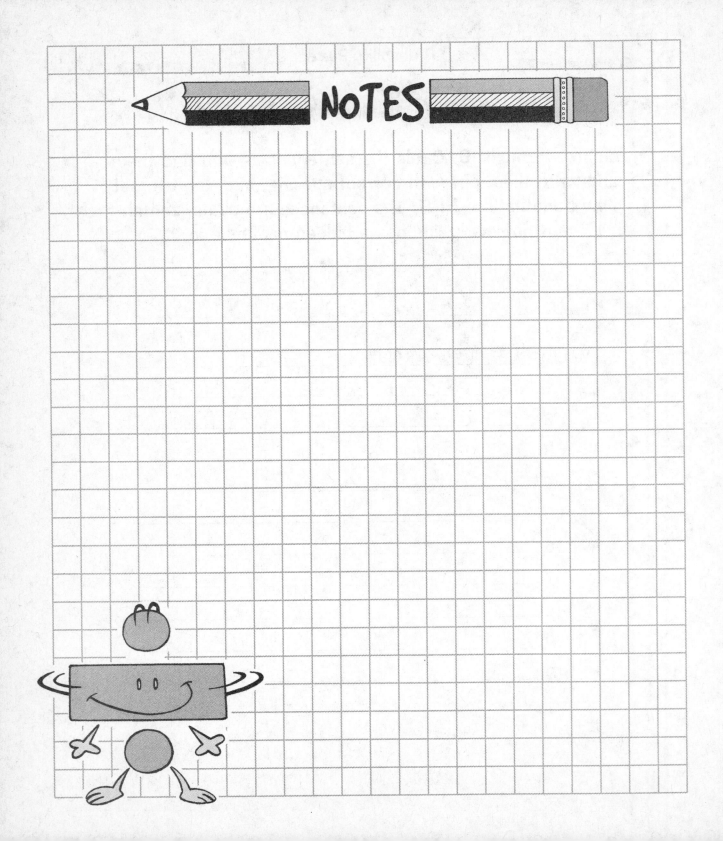

NOTES

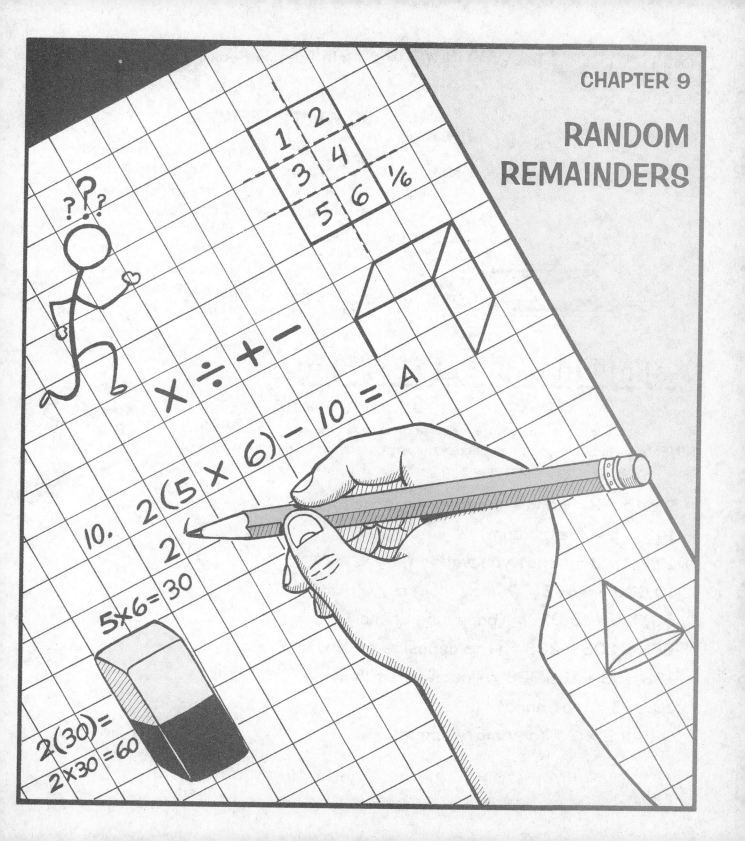

CHAPTER 9

RANDOM REMAINDERS

SO WHAT'S LEFT?

Y ou may already know what a **remainder** is: it's what's left over after a division problem. For example 35 ÷ 8 = 4 with a remainder of 3: 8 goes into 35 4 times, but since 4 × 8 = 32, there is still 3 left over.

The puzzles in this chapter are the remainder of the book—we've crammed it with fun activities that you didn't get a chance to see in any of the previous chapters.

S P E L L U L A T O R

Work out each problem with a calculator. When you are through figuring, turn the calculator upside down to read the answer to the clue in parentheses.
NOTE: Some calculators automatically display a decimal point with two zeros—ignore those, because it may make your answer difficult to read!

9,645 / 3 = (small, medium, or large) ....

142 × 5 = (petroleum) ....

1,879 × 3 = (what you walk on) ....

10,000 – 4,662 = (honey makers) ....

50,029 – 15,023 = (barnyard animal) ....

206 + 206 + 206 = (the opposite of tiny) ....

188,308 + 188,308 = (laugh in a silly way) ....

10 + 13 = (not hard) ....

926 × 2 × 2 = (an empty space) ....

Calling Code

Sam is calling his friends to invite them to a party. Using the phone keypad as a decoder, figure out the names of the people invited. Each phone button has several letters on it, so be sure to look for the number after the slash. It tells you if the letter is in the second or third space. For example, 2/2 = B. A number with no slash after it means the letter is in the first space.

1. 4/3-6-2   6/2-8/2-8-8

2. 3/3-7/2-2-6/2-5/2

   6/2   7/3-8-3/2-4/3-6/2

3. 8-3/2-3   3/2   2/2-3/2-2-7/2

4. 8-2-3/3-3/3-9/3   7-8/2-5/3-5/3

5. 3-7/2-3/2-9   2   2/2-6/3-2-8

6. 7/3-8/2-6-6-3/2-7/2   8-4/3-6-3/2

7. 7/3-2-6/2-8-2   2/3-5/3-2-8/2-7/3

NETWORK PUZZLES

Network puzzles require you to make sense of a network that is presented to you. One of the most famous network puzzles is the **Seven Bridges of Königsberg** problem.

In Königsberg, Germany (now Kaliningrad, Russia), there was an island in the middle of a river that flowed through the city. After the river passed around the island, it separated into two branches. Seven bridges were built so that the people of the city could move around.

WORDS 2 KNOW

network: An interconnected structure, group, or system of points and lines. There are many types of networks: computer networks, railroad networks, bridge networks, Internet networks, and so on.

A map of the center of Königsberg looks like this:

Can you walk around the city and only cross each bridge once?

Try it. Trace the map of the city on a sheet of paper and "walk" around the city with a pencil so that you trace over each bridge once and only once without lifting your pencil.

If the original problem seems hard, sometimes it helps to solve a simpler version:

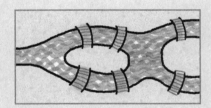

Suppose they built six bridges in Königsberg. Could you walk around the city and only cross each bridge once?

Why is this question easier? How is it different from the first question?

Q: What's the matter with the math book?
A: It has problems.

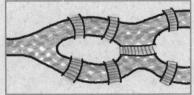

An Approach That Makes Sense

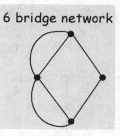

7 bridge network   6 bridge network

Here's a method to help you with any number of bridge network problems—or any network problems, for that matter. First, turn the city map into a diagram, where each circle is a piece of land and each line is a bridge.

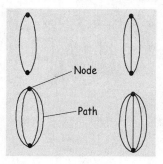

Node

Path

Each dot of land is called a node. You start and end at a node (not always ending at the place you started) and travel along the lines that connect them (the paths).

Here is the general rule for solving a network. You look at each node and count how many paths lead out of that node. An even node has an even number of paths leading out of it. An odd node has an odd number of paths. A network can be solved (traced without lifting a pencil and crossing each path exactly once) if the number of odd nodes is 0, 1, or 2.

Practice Solving Networks

For each of the following network puzzles, first figure out if it can be solved by counting the number of odd nodes. If it can be solved, then mark it with arrows to show how to trace around it and cross each path exactly once.

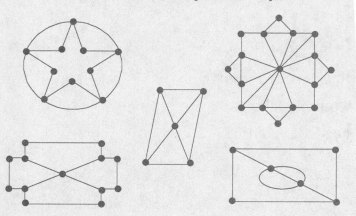

HEE
HEE
HEE

FUN FACT

It's Perfect!

Have you ever heard of "perfect" numbers? They are whole numbers that are equal to the sum of their proper divisors. For example, 6 is a perfect number because 6 = 1 + 2 + 3. Other perfect numbers include 28, 496, 8128, 33550336, 8589869056, 137438691328, 2305843008139952128, and 26584559 9156983174465469261595384 2176. How do you think they calculated that one?

Number Patterns

See if you can figure out the next number in each of these eight sequences:

Sequence 1: 4, 6, 8, 10, 12, ☐   Sequence 5: 3, 6, 12, 24, 48, ☐

Sequence 2: 5, 10, 15, 20, 25, ☐   Sequence 6: 1, 3, 9, 27, 81, ☐

Sequence 3: 3, 7, 11, 15, 19, ☐   Sequence 7: 1, 1, 2, 3, 5, 8, 13, ☐

Sequence 4: 4, 9, 16, 25, 36, ☐   Sequence 8: 1, 2, 6, 24, 120, ☐

HOPSCOTCH MATH

Bet you've never played hopscotch this way! Use the numbered hopscotch board here and for each "turn" add up the numbers in the spaces on which you hop.

• For example, on your first turn you would "hop" over number 1, so don't count it. • As you keep hopping up the board, add 2+3+4+5+6+7+8+9+10. • Turn around and hop back down the board adding 9+8+7+6+5+4+3+2 for a total of 98 points. • On your second turn you would hop on 1, hop over 2 (so don't count it), and keep on going.

QUESTION:
How many turns would it take to get 380 points?

COLOR MY WORLD

In 1893, Francis Guthrie, a student, wondered whether any map could be colored with four colors or fewer—to illustrate the borders, countries that share a border must be different colors.

Try to color the map of Africa using only four colors. This may be harder than it sounds, but it isn't impossible! **HINT:** Choose one color and fill in as many countries as possible. Then move to the second color, the third, and—finally—the fourth. Countries that share a border cannot be the same color. ▶

The Burden of Proof

This seemingly simple question perplexed mathematicians for years. In 1976, two mathematicians, Appel and Haken, wrote a computer program to determine if any map could be colored with four colors. The program took over 1,200 hours to run, but finally verified that only four colors are needed to color any map.

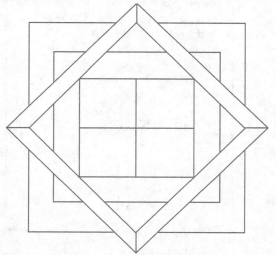

Crazy Quilting

◀ This quilting figure isn't a map, but the same idea is true—you should be able to color all the sections using only four colors, so that no two sections that touch are the same color. **HINT:** This puzzle is easier if you start from the middle and work your way out.

AN UNSOLVED MYSTERY

The puzzles in this book have answers, but there are some famous mathematical puzzles to which no one knows the answer yet. Maybe you will solve a famous unsolved puzzle.

One such puzzle is known as the **Goldbach's Conjecture.** The conjecture is as follows: **All even numbers greater than 2 can be written as the sum of two prime numbers.** (Remember, a prime number is one that can only be divided by 1 and itself.)

No one has proved that this is always true or disproved it by finding an example that doesn't work (a counter-example). Here are examples that illustrate Goldbach's Conjecture:

6 = 3 + 3
8 = 3 + 5
10 = 3 + 7 or 5 + 5 (there may be more than one answer)

Can you find two prime numbers that add up to the following even numbers? (You may want to use the prime numbers you found in Chapter 3.)

12 = _____ + _____   34 = _____ + _____

14 = _____ + _____   46 = _____ + _____

16 = _____ + _____   58 = _____ + _____

20 = _____ + _____   60 = _____ + _____

24 = _____ + _____

Young Math Geniuses

Solving famous puzzles is not only for mathematicians with a lot of education. In 1995, two ninth-graders found an original solution to this problem: Divide any line segment into a set number of equal parts using only a compass and straightedge. Variations of this problem date back to the time of Euclid (300 B.C.). Find out about their solution at *www.gfacademy.org/GLaD*.

Around, and Around, and Around We Go

This triple whirligig pattern, or "triskele," is a very old and powerful symbol. Since the ancient Celtic people of Ireland thought that the number 3 was both sacred and magical, they may have believed that this symbol brought good luck and protection from evil. Sometimes the artist would add tiny lines or dots to make the pattern look like an animal, a flower, or a human face.

As you wind your way through this mysterious triskele, find a bird in a nest, an elf in a pointy hat, a fish, two snakes looking at each other, and a bird with a big beak.

START

END

That's Just about Right

Take a wild guess at how many daisies are in this field. Write your wild guess here: _____

Here's a handy trick that will help you to get close to the correct number of daisies.

1. Use a ruler and a brightly colored marker to divide the picture into a number of equal sized boxes. The boxes don't have to be perfectly square, and it doesn't matter how many boxes you make, as long as they're the same size.
2. Count the flower heads (not the stems) in one of the boxes. Count flowers that are more than half in the box as one flower.
3. Now multiply the number of flowers in one box by the total number of boxes on the picture.

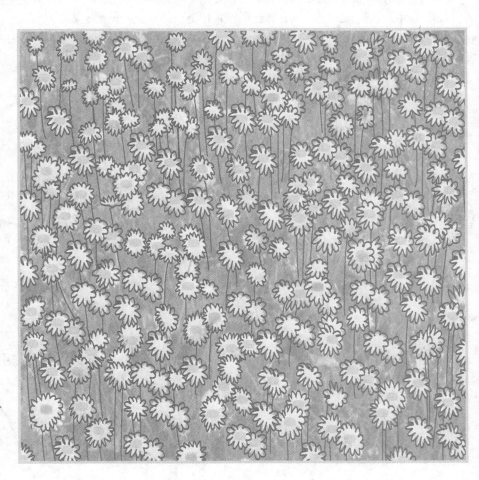

This answer is based on reasoning and is called an estimate. An estimate is still a guess, but it's an educated guess, not just a wild one! Write your estimate of the number of flowers here: _____

How do your two answers compare?

The Very Last cross-Number Puzzle

Well, you've come to the end of the book.
But before you go on your way, here is one last cross-number puzzle you can enjoy!

Across

1. If "a cat has nine lives," then how many lives do nine cats have?
3. How many cards are in a full deck?
5. The number that is two numbers after 5, three times in a row!
7. How much is seven sevens?
8. How many days are in a year?
10. How many Dalmatians are in that classic movie?
11. How many hours are in a day?
12. What's between 5 and 9?
15. It takes eight rows of eight checkers to fill a checkerboard. How many checkers is that?
16. How many states are in the United States?

Down

1. A score is twenty years. How many years is "four score and seven"?
2. XVII in Arabic numbers.
3. How would you see "quarter to six" on a digital clock?
4. A month can have this many days, but not often.
6. What's an early bedtime?
9. This number is a palindrome.
10. A dozen dozens is called a "gross"! If you have a gross of pencils, how many pencils do you have?
11. Take an unlucky number and double it.
13. How many pennies equal three quarters?
14. What's left of a dollar if you spend a dime and two nickels?

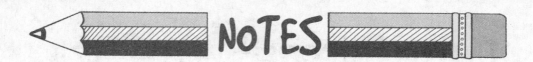

Glossary of Math Terms

Arabic numerals

A numeral system that relies on ten digits—0, 1, 2, 3, 4, 5, 6, 7, 8, and 9. The Arabic numerals are what we use today.

Averages

There are three ways to calculate the average. The **mean** is what you get if you add up all the values and divide the total by the number of values. This is typically what people mean when they use the word **average**. The **median** of a set of values is the value in the middle of the set when the set is written in order. The **mode** of a set of values is the value that occurs most often. Mode is usually used as the average when the values are not numbers, like eye or hair color.

Binary system

A numeral system that uses 1 and 0, where 1 represents "on" and 0 represents "off." Our computers rely on the binary system.

Calculate

This term originated from the Greek word *kalyx*—pebble or small stone—because a long time ago, Greeks used small stones to do simple calculations.

Centi–

1/100.

Deci–

1/10.

Deka–

10.

Digit

A number—but also a word for "finger." Coincidence? We think not. It's very likely that the first people to start counting used their fingers—just as little kids continue to do today.

Fibonacci series: A series of numbers that begin with 1, 1, 2, 3, 5, 8, 13, and so on, where the two first numbers add up to the third (1+1=2), the second and third numbers add up to the fourth (1+2=3), and so on. This sequence was devised by Leonardo Pisano (Fibonacci), a mathematician who lived in Pisa, Italy, between 1170 and 1250.

Geometry

A study of physical shapes. Literally, **geometry** means "to measure the Earth."

Hecto–

100.

Irrational

In mathematics, irrational numbers are those that cannot be represented as a fraction—they go on forever and ever with no repeating pattern.

Kilo–

1,000.

Mathematics

Based on the Greek word *manthanein* (to learn), mathematics measures and describes the world with numbers and symbols.

Milli–

1/1,000.

Network

An interconnected structure, group, or system of points and lines. There are many types of networks: computer networks, railroad networks, bridge networks, Internet networks, and so on.

Obelus

The symbol "÷" used to indicate division. The word comes from the Greek word *obelos*, for spit or spike, a pointed stick used for cooking. The symbol has been used as a division symbol since around 1650.

Pi (p)

This number represents the ratio of circumference (the distance around the circle) and diameter (the distance across the circle). This number is the same for all circles, no matter what their size.

Polygon

A geometrical figure with three or more sides. The term **polygon** is from the Greek roots *poli* (many) and *gonus* (knees). Greeks thought of a polygon as a shape of many angles, which look like bent knees.

Prime number

A number that is divisible by just two different numbers, 1 and itself. Seven is prime because it can only be divided by 1 and 7. Eight is not a prime number because besides 1 and 8, it is also divisible by 2 and 4. The word **prime** comes from *primus*, the Latin word for "first."

Probability

The chances of something happening—actually, the ratio of the number of times it could happen compared to the number of possible things that could happen. For example, when you throw dice, you have 1/6 chances of getting each particular number.

Roman numerals

Numerals I (1), V (5), X (10), L (50), C (100), D (500), M (1,000), and so on, which were invented by the Romans and are still used today on clocks and in a few other cases.

Solar system

The sun, nine planets that revolve around it—Mercury, Venus, Earth, Mars, Jupiter, Saturn, Uranus, Neptune, and Pluto—as well as all of their respective moons, comets, and asteroids.

Solidus

The slanted bar "/" used for fractions and division. During the Roman Empire, the solidus was a gold coin. On the reverse of the coin was a picture of a spear bearer, with the spear going from lower left to upper right. This spear became the symbol for fractions and division.

Tallies

Simple lines that each represent one object and are used for simple counting.

Read All about It!

Anno's Mysterious Multiplying Jar

by Masaichiro and Mitsumasa Anno (Philomel Books, 1983)

Counting on Frank

by Rod Clement (Gareth Stevens Publishing, 1991) explores how you and your imagination can make counting wild!

Easy Origami

by John Montroll (Dover Publications, 1992) shows you how to make basic origami folds and how to make fish, birds, boats, and windmills.

Grandfather Tang's Story, A Tale Told with Tangrams

by Ann Tompert (Crown Publishers, 1990). Changing tangram pictures tell the story about two foxes and a dangerous game that might get one of them killed.

The Greedy Triangle

by Marilyn Burns (Scholastic, 1994). What if a dissatisfied triangle wanted more sides? In this story, a triangle changes into a quadrilateral, then a pentagon, then a hexagon, and keeps growing. Will it ever be happy? Find out by reading *The Greedy Triangle!*

How Much Is a Million?

by David M. Schwartz (Scholastic, 1985) shows a million, a billion, and a trillion in pictures of children, goldfish, and stars. If you can imagine a million, then how much bigger is a billion?

If You Made a Million

by David M. Schwartz (Scholastic, 1989). Read this book if you are curious to explore what a million dollars looks like and what it could buy!

Is a Blue Whale the Biggest Thing There Is?

by Robert E. Wells (Albert Whitman & Company, 1993) stretches your mind's idea about how big is *really* big, from the blue whale to the size of the universe.

Jumanji

by Chris Van Allsburg (Houghton Mifflin Company, 1981). What if a roll of dice and a move on the game board was real? Read and figure out the probability of the next move. This book was made into a movie—did you see it?

The King's Chessboard

by David Birch (Puffin Pied Piper, 1988). When a wise man asks the king to double his gift of rice every day, can the king really grant the wise man's request? Learn how the power of doubling convinces the king that the humble wise man has a lesson worthy even of kings.

Math Curse

by Jon Scieszka and Lane Smith (Viking, 1995) imagines what it would be like if everything you look at turns into a math problem and you didn't like math. In this funny story, the clever girl eventually breaks the math curse.

Origami, Plain and Simple

by Robert Neale and Thomas Hull (St. Martin's Press, 1994) is a great book for beginners—it even shows you how to make an entire chess set from paper.

Roman Numerals I to MM

by Arthur Geisert (Houghton Mifflin Company, 1996).

Sir Cumference and the First Round Table

by Cindy Neuschwander (Charlesbridge Publishing, 1997). In this fun tale, King Arthur's knights try out a variety of shapes for tables until a knight's son finds the best solution.

What's Smaller Than a Pygmy Shrew?

by Robert E. Wells (Albert Whitman & Company, 1995) can help you imagine how small is *really* small—down to a particle that is smaller than a molecule.

PUZZLE ANSWERS

page 2 • Roman Numerals

Answer: CLOCK

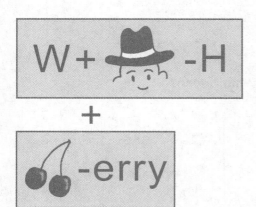

Answer: WATCH

page 4 • When in Rome

149	14	2660	922	1606	14	61
N	A	T	U	R	A	L

149	922	411	29	8	1606	751
N	U	M	B	E	R	S

page 5 • Hidden Numbers

1. I love my computer — when it works!
2. Beth reeked of smoke after sitting by the campfire.
3. My mother likes to weigh tomatoes on every scale in the store.
4. Annie was even early for school last week!
5. We can stuff our dirty backpacks in your tent.
6. We like the mirrored maze room at the fun park.

page 6 • Practice Your Digits

START				
3	3	4	2	3
4	1	1	2	2
2	4	3	1	4
2	3	1	4	3
4	2	1	2	E END

START					
4	2	1	2	3	4
3	3	4	2	3	4
4	2	4	2	4	3
3	2	1	3	2	4
2	2	4	2	3	4
4	1	4	1	2	E END

page 7 • On or Off?

T-O-O-T-H T-H-I-R-T-Y

PUZZLE ANSWERS

pages 10–11 • **Making Sense of the Irrational**

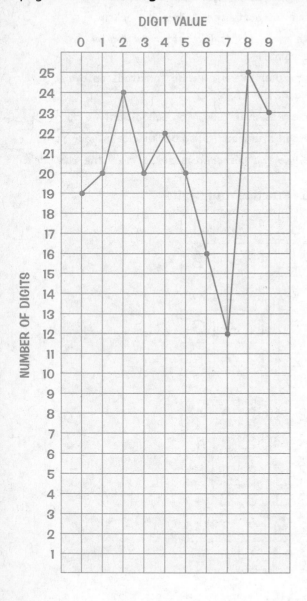

DIGIT VALUE

NUMBER OF DIGITS

page 12 • **Let's Get Packing**

1. Call Kelly Short for directions to State park.

2. Buy sun block and bug spray.

3. Check the flashlight batteries.

4. Fill water bottles, make snacks, and get chocolate!

5. Pack ponchos and extra socks.

6. Find binoculars and bird books.

page 13 • **See What I Mean?**

page 16 • **Clock Math**

$10 + 12 =$ T

$3 + 4 =$ O

$10 + 9 =$ O

$1 - 3 =$ T

$5 - 2 =$ H

$11 + 4 =$ H

$8 + 3 =$ U

$11 - 3 =$ R

$11 - 1 =$ T

$12 + 12 =$ Y

PUZZLE ANSWERS

page 18 • **Numbers with Direction**

14	21	13	2	5	18
N	U	M	B	E	R

12	9	14	5
L	I	N	E

page 20 • **Connect the Dots**

Do in order	Addition	Subtraction
A.	-3 + -5 = -8	-3 - -5 = 2
B.	-4 + 2 = -2	4 - -8 = 2
C.	-1 + 5 = 4	5 - 2 = 3
D.	4 + -8 = -4	- 4 - -2 = -2
E.	7 + -2 = 5	7 - -2 = 9
F.	-3 + 3 = 0	-2 - -2 = 0
G.	3 + 4 = 7	-3 - 4 = -7
H.	-2 + -2 = -4	-1 -1 = -2

page 21 • **Magic Squares**

There is more than one way to complete the magic squares, but the solutions will be similar. Here is one way of solving each magic square.

Magic Square 5

8	3	4
1	5	9
6	7	2

Magic Square 10

16	6	8
2	10	18
12	14	4

Magic Square 9

15	5	7
1	9	17
11	13	3

Magic Square 0

3	-2	-1
-4	0	4
1	2	-3

Magic Square 1

4	-1	0
-3	1	5
2	3	-2

Magic Square 4X4

16	2	3	13
5	11	10	8
9	7	6	12
4	14	15	1

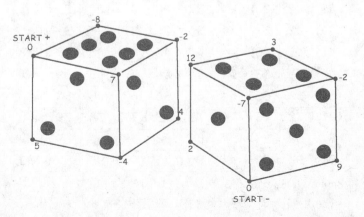

pages 24–27 •
Solve a Cross-Number Puzzle

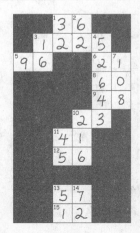

125

PUZZLE ANSWERS

page 28 • Cross Sums

9↓	24↓		27↓	13↓
5→ 4	1	12→	5	7
11→ 5	6	6↓ 15→	9	6
17→ 15↓ 3	6	8		11↓
16→ 7	9	12→	4	8
13→ 8	5	4↓	1	3

page 29 • It's My Favorite

I LOVE TO ADD

page 35 • Multiplication Boxes

-4	5	-20
-9	6	-54
36	30	1080

7	10	70
11	-1	-11
77	-10	-770

7	3	21
-5	-2	10
-35	-6	210

-3	6	-18
7	-8	-56
-21	-48	1008

page 36 • Musical Math

$5\overline{)95} = 19$ $4\overline{)72} = 18$ $3\overline{)87} = 29$ $6\overline{)84} = 14$

$7\overline{)175} = 25$ $3\overline{)141} = 47$

$8\overline{)168} = 21$ $6\overline{)264} = 44$

$8\overline{)264} = 33$ $6\overline{)186} = 31$

Y 31	A 45	U 47	O 16	R 19	N 12	Y 21	M 29
R 44	E 13	B 15	R 33	M 25	G 18	A 22	W 14

What comes before a tuba?
Answer: A one-ba!

page 41 • The Sieve of Eratosthenes

	②	③	4	⑤	6	⑦	8	9	10
⑪	12	⑬	14	15	16	⑰	18	⑲	20
21	22	㉓	24	25	26	27	28	㉙	30
㉛	32	33	34	35	36	㊲	38	39	40
㊶	42	㊸	44	45	46	㊼	48	49	50
51	52	㊾	54	55	56	57	58	㊾	60
61	62	63	64	65	66	㊻	68	69	70
71	72	73	74	75	76	77	78	79	80
81	82	83	84	85	86	87	88	89	90
91	92	93	94	95	96	97	98	99	100

Prime Numbers: 2, 3, 5, 7, 11, 13, 17, 19, 23, 29, 31, 37, 41, 43, 47, 53, 59, 61, 67, 71, 73, 79, 83, 89, 97

PUZZLE ANSWERS

page 45 • Squares and Radicals

$5^2 = 25$; $6^2 = 36$; $7^2 = 49$; $8^2 = 64$; $9^2 = 81$; $10^2 = 100$; $11^2 = 121$; $12^2 = 144$; $13^2 = 169$; $14^2 = 196$; $15^2 = 225$; $16^2 = 256$; $17^2 = 289$; $18^2 = 324$; $19^2 = 361$; $20^2 = 400$

page 46 • Goofy Gardener

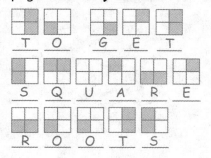

TO GET SQUARE ROOTS

page 47 • A Radical Sign

$\sqrt{9} = 3$; $\sqrt{16} = 4$; $\sqrt{25} = 5$; $\sqrt{49} = 7$; $\sqrt{64} = 8$; $\sqrt{81} = 9$; $\sqrt{100} = 10$.

page 48 • On Your Mark!

$\sqrt{9}$ **3** to get ready,

$-3 + 4$ **1** for the money,

2^2 **4** to go!

$4 \div 2$ **2** for the show,

1 for the money,
2 for the show,
3 to get ready,
4 to go!

page 50 • How Four Can You Go?

$2 = (4 \times 4 \div 4) \div \sqrt{4}$

$3 = (4 + 4 + 4) \div 4$

$4 = \sqrt{(4 \times 4 \times 4)} - 4$

$5 = (4 \times 4 + 4) \div 4$

$6 = (4 + 4 + 4) \div \sqrt{4}$

$7 = 4 + [(4 + \sqrt{4}) \div \sqrt{4}]$

$8 = 4 \times 4 \div 4 + 4$

$9 = 4 + 4 + (4 \div 4)$

$10 = 4 \times 4 - 4 - \sqrt{4}$

$11 = 44 \div (\sqrt{4} + \sqrt{4})$

$12 = \sqrt{(4 \times 4 \times 4)} + 4$

$13 = (44 \div 4) + \sqrt{4}$

$14 = 4 + 4 + 4 + \sqrt{4}$

$15 = (4 \times 4) - (4 \div 4)$

page 51 • Your Number's Up

1 ONE STEP AT A TIME / HOLE IN ONE / A LONELY NUMBER
2 TEA FOR TWO / DICE IN A MONOPOLY GAME
3 LITTLE PIGS / THREE MUSKETEERS
4 QUARTERS IN A DOLLAR / 4 PRIVET DRIVE (The Dursleys' address in *Harry Potter*)
5 POINTS ON A STAR / OLYMPIC RINGS / SCHOOL DAYS IN A WEEK
6 HALF A DOZEN / LEGS ON AN INSECT
7 DWARVES WITH SNOW WHITE / DAYS IN A WEEK
8 ARMS ON AN OCTOPUS / OUNCES IN A CUP / FIGURE 8 IN ICE SKATING / EIGHT SIDES ON A STOP SIGN
9 CAT LIVES / PLANETS IN OUR SOLAR SYSTEM
10 FINGERS OR TOES / COMMANDMENTS
11 PLAYERS ON A FOOTBALL OR SOCCER TEAM / APOLLO 11 MISSION TO THE MOON
12 MONTHS IN A YEAR / NUMBERS ON A CLOCK FACE
13 AN UNLUCKY NUMBER / STRIPES ON THE U.S. FLAG
14 FEBRUARY 14 IS VALENTINE'S DAY
15 MINUTES IN A QUARTER OF AN HOUR
16 OUNCES IN A POUND
17 TITLE OF A TEEN MAGAZINE / AMERICAN REVOLUTION STARTED IN **17**76
18 HOLES ON A GOLF COURSE / AN AGE WHEN YOU ARE OLD ENOUGH TO VOTE
19 *19*84 (title of a book) / BUILDING 19 (a discount store)
20 FINGERS AND TOES (all together) / *20 THOUSAND LEAGUES UNDER THE SEA* (title of a book)
21 ANOTHER NAME FOR THE GAME OF BLACKJACK / THE CENTURY WE ARE IN
22 FEBRUARY 22 IS GEORGE WASHINGTON'S BIRTHDAY
23 MICHAEL JORDAN'S NUMBER / CHROMOSOMES IN A HUMAN BEING
24 HOURS IN A DAY / TWO DOZEN
25 DECEMBER 25 IS CHRISTMAS DAY / A SILVER ANNIVERSARY
50 U.S. STATES / STARS ON THE U.S. FLAG
100 "ONE HUNDRED BOTTLES OF BEER ON THE WALL" SONG / PERFECT SCORE ON A TEST

PUZZLE ANSWERS

page 54 • Shape Changers

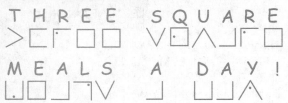

THREE SQUARE

MEALS A DAY!

page 55 • Six-Sided Math

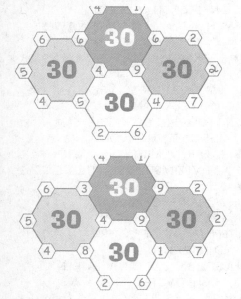

page 56 • Hide in Plain Sight

page 57 • Life of the Party

1	2	3	4	5	6	7	8	9
P	O	I	N	T	L	E	S	S

page 58 • Going Around in Circles

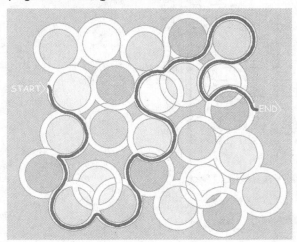

page 61 • The Last Straw

Tape the tips of three straws together to form a triangle that lies flat on the table. Now, take the remaining three straws and tape them so that one stands upright from each of the three corners. Finally, lean the three straws toward the center and tape all three tips together so that you have an open pyramid. This is called a "tetrahedron," and it is made up of one triangle lying flat on the table plus three more triangles for the upright side.

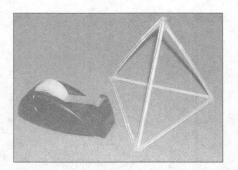

PUZZLE ANSWERS

page 62 • **Get to the Point!**

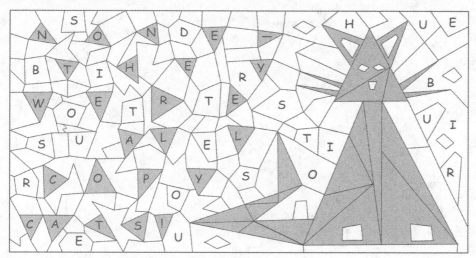

Answer: None — they were all copy cats!

pages 64–65 • **On a Treasure Hunt**

The Windy Hill

1. *Her father was afraid of ghosts and wouldn't want his money close to the cemetery.* Cross out the cemetery.
2. *Cash Steele did not like small dark places either.* Cross out mine shaft, well, and cave.
3. *If he buried the money, it would be to the north of his cabin.* There are no underground hiding places left north of the cabin, so he must not have buried his money. Cross out dino bones.
4. *If he hid it aboveground, it would be south of the cabin.* Both the barn and the Lone Pine are north of the cabin, so cross those out.
5. *If he didn't hide it in the well, then he didn't hide it in the windmill, either.* He didn't hide it in the well (you've already crossed it out), so you can cross out the windmill as well. Now, the only other hiding place left is Windy Hill, which is the answer.

page 66 • **A Square Deal**

4	2	4	3	1	3	4	2	4
2	1	2	4	3	4	2	1	2
1	2	4	3	2	3	4	2	3
3	4	3	2	1	2	3	4	1
4	3	2	1	**4**	1	2	1	2
3	4	3	2	1	2	3	4	1
2	1	2	4	3	2	3	4	2	3
2	1	2	4	1	4	2	1	2
4	2	4	1	3	1	4	2	4

page 66 • **The Domino Effect**

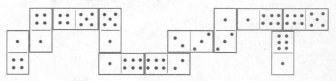

Dominoes work by matching the open numbers, so that a 1 goes next to a 1, a 2 next to a 2, and so on.

129

PUZZLE ANSWERS

page 67 • **Picture This**

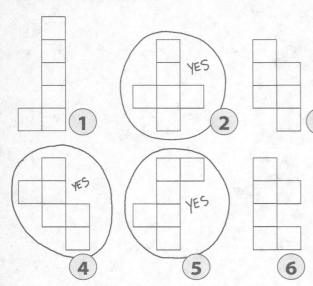

page 75 • **Star Power**

pages 72–73 • **Not by a Long Shot**
Giraffe

pages 76–77 • **A Weighty Matter**
Blue whale

page 74 • **Hink Pinks**

1. Pile of games that weighs 2,000 lbs. FUN TON
2. 5,280 foot grin MILE SMILE
3. Two pastries that are each 12 inches long SWEET FEET
4. Very difficult 3 feet HARD YARD
5. Rubber ball that weighs 16 ounces ROUND POUND
6. 28.4 grams that jumps quickly OUNCE POUNCE
7. Urgent message that weighs 2.2 pounds KILOGRAM TELEGRAM

page 78 • **Measuring Your ZZZs**

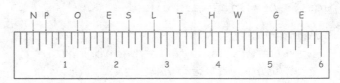

$\underline{T}_{3\frac{2}{8}}$ $\underline{O}_{1.25}$ $\underline{S}_{2.25}$ $\underline{E}_{1\frac{7}{8}}$ $\underline{E}_{5\frac{5}{8}}$ $\underline{H}_{3\frac{7}{8}}$ $\underline{O}_{1.25}$ $\underline{W}_{4\frac{3}{8}}$ $\underline{L}_{2.75}$ $\underline{O}_{1\frac{1}{4}}$ $\underline{N}_{\frac{3}{8}}$ $\underline{G}_{5\frac{1}{8}}$

$\underline{S}_{2\frac{1}{4}}$ $\underline{H}_{3\frac{7}{8}}$ $\underline{E}_{1\frac{7}{8}}$ $\underline{S}_{2\frac{2}{8}}$ $\underline{L}_{2\frac{3}{4}}$ $\underline{E}_{1\frac{7}{8}}$ $\underline{P}_{\frac{5}{8}}$ $\underline{T}_{3\frac{2}{8}}$

page 79 •
Lost Billions

```
B I L L I O N N S B B I
B I L S B S N O I L I B
I B S S N B I L L O N S
L S N N B O B I L L N O
L N I O I I I B B O B I
I O O I L B O L I B I L
I L L O B S I L O B I
O L L O N L B O I S L
N L I B I L I O B B I I
S I B L I B O B I L I B
I B L B B I L O O N S I
O B B I L I O O N S O L
```

PUZZLE ANSWERS

page 80 • Googols of Fun

1 7·15·15·7·15·12   8·1·19
   A G O O G O L   H A S

15·14·5   8·21·14·4·18·5·4
O N E   H U N D R E D

26·5·18·15·19
Z E R O S

page 81 • On Your Toes

SHE · ADDS · TWO · FEET

pages 84–85 • Logical Math

1. The *other one* is a nickel!
2. 99 + (9 ÷ 9) = 100
3. 30 ÷ 15 = 2 and 2 + 10 = 12. Note: 30 *divided by* half is not the same as 30 *divided in* half.
4. You have the three apples you took away.
5. "A pie in the face."
6. "One in a million."
7. "Six of one, half a dozen of another."
8. He weighs meat!

page 86 • Moving Around

Gary is moving to Boston, Harry is moving to Dallas, Larry is moving to Chicago, Mary is moving to Atlanta.

page 87 • Taming Dragons

	Day 1	Day 2	Day 3	Day 4
Ruby	Smokey	Spitfire	Forktail	Blaze
Jade	Forktail	Smokey	Blaze	Spitfire
Sapphire	Blaze	Forktail	Spitfire	Smokey
Topaz	Spitfire	Blaze	Smokey	Forktail

page 87 • The Marriage Proposal

Ruby can take out one pebble and "accidentally" drop it into the river. Then, she'll insist that the pebble was white. Since the other pebble in the purse is black, everyone has to assume that she dropped the white pebble—and she won't have to marry the sneaky prince!

pages 88–89 • In the Land of Confusion

Can you figure out who is a sage and who is a jester? Xavier and Zachary are sages, and Yale is a jester. Here is the explanation: Xavier must be a sage because if he were a jester, he would lie about it. Since Xavier is a sage, Yale is a jester—his claim that Xavier is lying is untrue. In turn, that means Zachary is telling the truth, so he is a sage.

Are the boy and girl sages and/or jesters, and what color hair does each one have? They are both jesters; the boy has red hair and the girl has black hair. If the third statement is true, then either the first or the second statement must be untrue; but that's impossible—either they are both true or both untrue, since one is a boy and the other is a girl. That means the boy is a jester, which means that he is the one who said, "I'm a girl." Therefore, the girl is also a jester, because she said, "I'm a boy."

PUZZLE ANSWERS

pages 88–89 • In the Land of Confusion, *continued*

What can you tell about him or his son? They are both sages. Let's look at it this way:

1. If the statement is true, then they are either both sages or jesters; since the father is telling the truth, they are both sages.

2. If the statement is false and the father is a jester, his son must be a sage, in which case the statement is not a lie, which means that the father cannot be a jester.

That means the only possible outcome is that they are both sages.

Immediately, the sages cried: "Imposter! Arrest that man!" Why? If the King were a sage, he would say the truth, "I'm a sage." If the King were a jester, he would lie and say, "I'm a sage." Since the King said, "I'm a jester," he is neither a sage nor a jester, and is not a citizen of the Land of Confusion.

pages 90–91 • Read the Numbers

CR8TV	1DRFL	42N8
7. CREATIVE	4. WONDERFUL	2. FORTUNATE
4EVRL8	I4GOT	10SNY1
6. FOREVER LATE	9. I FORGOT	12. TENNIS ANYONE?
H82W8	2BA	W8NC
8. HATE TO WAIT	1. TUBA	10. WAIT AND SEE
4CAST	10Q	SK8R
5. FORECAST	3. THANK YOU	11. SKATER

page 92 • Simple Symbols

$$
\begin{array}{r}
6\ 2\ 1 \\
-\ 4\ 1\ 1 \\
\hline
2\ 1\ 0
\end{array}
\qquad
\begin{array}{r}
2\ 1\ 6 \\
-\ 1\ 1\ 2 \\
\hline
1\ 0\ 4
\end{array}
$$

page 92 • Buying Numbers
The customer was buying numbers for her front door.

page 93 • I Can't Find It!

```
1 2 2 1 3 1 2 3 5
2 2 3 3 1 2 1 4 1
1 2 1 2 5 2 2 1 2
2 3 1 4 3 1 4 2 5
1 2 3 4 2 3 3 4 4
4 1 5 2 1 2 1 3 3
5 3 4 1 2 4 4 5 5
1 2 2 1 3 4 5 1 2
3 1 1 2 4 3 3 2 1
```

page 93 • I Found It!

Students	# of books each student found
Jasmine	3
Katlyn	1
Josh	4
Ethan	5
TOTAL number of puzzle books found	13

page 98 • Who Owns That Car?
Look at the license plate upside down, and you'll see that the numbers spell out *OLLIE LEE*.

PUZZLE ANSWERS

page 99 • Even and Odd

×	1	2	3	4	5
1	1	(2)	3	(4)	5
2	(2)	(4)	(6)	(8)	(10)
3	3	(6)	9	(12)	15
4	(4)	(8)	(12)	(16)	(20)
5	5	(10)	15	(20)	25

page 100 • Get Out of Here

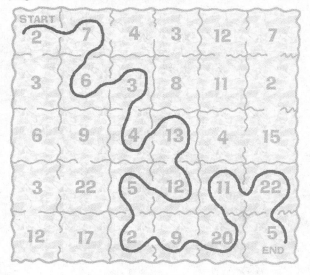

page 101 • An Average Day

One of the averages above is a mode. Which one is it? Average ice-cream flavor

pages 102–103 • Hidden Numbers, Etc.

```
B U T T E R H Y T F L Y T O P 7 3 Y R E S
T H E 2 (I O F 1 0 E A T H E R E) W E 9 S H
B E (P U T A P E 9 A C H B A G) W H E T 2 M
W H E N I 8 A N Y T R E B M K 9 0 4 V A T
7 O U R (W 8 H E A P P L E S P L E A S E) 8
(I T I 7 N O T O D D) I F 1 C B 2 B N 3 M O
B O P N E S 5 9 Y (S E E I 5 G O T M A I L)
M Y C A T (W H A T I 4 P H 1 R I N G S) R I
W H Y 7 J I M L P O T T E R S R E W 5 D U
T (T H E P O N D I S F I L L E D W I 3 D S)
V I T A M I 4 (T H A 2 U L D B E N I C E) K
N Y T H R T H I S I S A 4 A S T Y J I O B
6 T H E (S H E I S T O 1 A R T H E E D G E)
(H E H A S A B A R 9 A S T C O N C O R D) H
B U T I 6 (D O N 2 R R Y B E H A P P Y) P Y
```

SAMPLE: I of(ten) eat here.

1. Put a pen in each bag.
2. Weigh the apples, please.
3. It is even, not odd.
4. See if I've got mail.
5. What if our phone rings?
6. The pond is filled with reeds.
7. That would be nice!
8. She is too near the edge!
9. He has a barn in East Concord.
10. Don't worry, be happy!

page 106 • Spellulator

9,645 / 3 = (small, medium, or large)	3215, SIZE
142 × 5 = (petroleum)	710, OIL
1,879 × 3 = (what you walk on)	5637, LEGS
10,000 – 4,662 = (honey makers)	5338, BEES
50,029 – 15,023 = (barnyard animal)	35006, GOOSE
206 + 206 + 206 = (the opposite of tiny)	618, BIG
188,308 + 188,308 = (laugh in a silly way)	376616, GIGGLE
10 + 13 = (not hard)	23, EZ
926 × 2 × 2 = (an empty space)	3704, HOLE

PUZZLE ANSWERS

page 107 • Calling Code

1. IMA NUTT
2. FRANK N STEIN
3. TED E BEAR
4. TAFFY PULL
5. DREW A BOAT
6. SUMMER TIME
7. SANTA CLAUS

page 109 • Practice Solving Networks

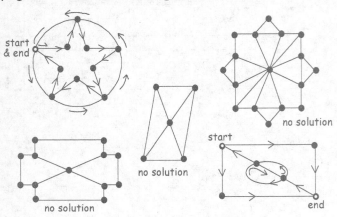

page 110 • Number Patterns

Sequence 1: $+2 = $ **14**
Sequence 2: $+5 = $ **30**
Sequence 3: $+4 = $ **23**
Sequence 4: $+5, +7, +9, +11, +13 = $ **49**
Sequence 5: $\times 2 = $ **96**
Sequence 6: $\times 3 = $ **243**
Sequence 7: 1, 1, 2, 3, 5, 8, 13 : $1 + 1 = 2; 1 + 2 = 3; 2 + 3 = 5; 3 + 5 = 8; 5 + 8 = 13; 8 + 13 = $ **21**
Sequence 8: 1, 2, 6, 24, 120 : $1 \times 2 = 2; 2 \times 3 = 6; 6 \times 4 = 24; 24 \times 5 = 120; 120 \times 6 = $ **720**

page 110 • Hopscotch Math

Turn One = 98 points
Turn Two = 96 points
Turn Three = 94 points
Turn Four = 92 points
Add all four turns together to get 380.

page 111 • Color My World

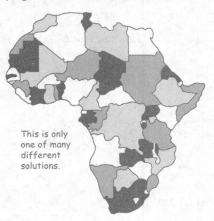

This is only one of many different solutions.

page 111 • Crazy Quilting

There are several ways you can color this pattern—this is just one way of doing it.

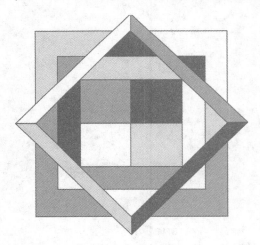

page 112 • An Unsolved Mystery

$12 = 5 + 7$	$34 = 31 + 3$
$14 = 11 + 3$	$46 = 23 + 23$
$16 = 11 + 5$	$58 = 53 + 5$
$20 = 13 + 7$	$60 = 53 + 7$
$24 = 11 + 13$	

PUZZLE ANSWERS

page 113 • **Around, and Around, and Around We Go**

page 115 • **The Very Last Cross-Number Puzzle**

1:8	2:1			3:5	4:2
5:7	7	6:7	7	7:4	9
		8:3	9:6	5	
	10:1	0	1		
11:2	4		12:6	13:7	14:8
15:6	4			16:5	0

page 114 • **That's Just about Right**
Answers will vary. We chose to divide the field of daisies into 24 boxes. There are about 10 daisies in every box. Therefore, we estimate that there are 240 daisies in the field pictured.

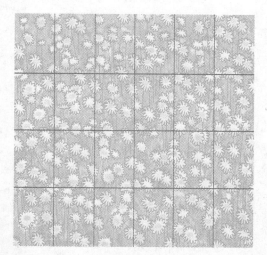

The Everything®  Series!

Packed with tons of information, activities, and puzzles, the Everything® Kids' books are perennial bestsellers that keep kids active and engaged.

Each book is two-color, 8" x 9¼", and 144 pages.

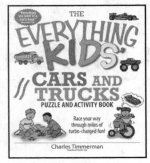

The Everything® Kids' Cars and
Trucks Puzzle and Activity Book
1-59337-703-7, $7.95

The Everything® Kids' First Spanish
Puzzle and Activity Book
1-59337-717-7, $7.95

The Everything® Kids' Learning
Spanish Book
1-59337-716-9, $7.95

The Everything® Kids'
Princess Puzzle and Activity Book
1-59337-704-5, $7.95

A silly, goofy, and undeniably icky addition to
the Everything® Kids' series . . .

The Everything® Kids'
GROSS
Series

Chock-full of sickening entertainment for hours of disgusting fun.

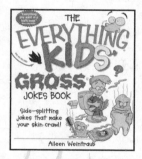

The Everything® Kids'
Gross Jokes Book
1-59337-448-8, $7.95

The Everything® Kids' Gross
Puzzle & Activity Book
1-59337-447-X, $7.95

The Everything® Kids'
Gross Mazes Book
1-59337-616-2, $7.95

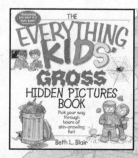

The Everything® Kids' Gross
Hidden Pictures Book
1-59337-615-4, $7.95

Other Everything® Kids' Titles Available

The Everything® Kids' Animal Puzzle & Activity Book
1-59337-305-8

The Everything® Kids' Baseball Book, 4th Ed.
1-59337-614-6

The Everything® Kids' Bible Trivia Book
1-59337-031-8

The Everything® Kids' Bugs Book
1-58062-892-3

The Everything® Kids' Christmas Puzzle & Activity Book
1-58062-965-2

The Everything® Kids' Cookbook
1-58062-658-0

The Everything® Kids' Crazy Puzzles Book
1-59337-361-9

The Everything® Kids' Dinosaurs Book
1-59337-360-0

The Everything® Kids' Halloween Puzzle & Activity Book
1-58062-959-8

The Everything® Kids' Hidden Pictures Book
1-59337-128-4

The Everything® Kids' Horses Book
1-59337-608-1

The Everything® Kids' Joke Book
1-58062-686-6

The Everything® Kids' Knock Knock Book
1-59337-127-6

The Everything® Kids' Math Puzzles Book
1-58062-773-0

The Everything® Kids' Mazes Book
1-58062-558-4

The Everything® Kids' Money Book
1-58062-685-8

The Everything® Kids' Nature Book
1-58062-684-X

The Everything® Kids' Pirates Puzzle and Activity Book
1-59337-607-3

The Everything® Kids' Puzzle Book
1-58062-687-4

The Everything® Kids' Riddles & Brain Teasers Book
1-59337-036-9

The Everything® Kids' Science Experiments Book
1-58062-557-6

The Everything® Kids' Sharks Book
1-59337-304-X

The Everything® Kids' Soccer Book
1-58062-642-4

The Everything® Kids' Travel Activity Book
1-58062-641-6

All titles are $6.95 or $7.95 unless otherwise noted.

Available wherever books are sold!
To order, call 800-258-0929, or visit us at *www.adamsmedia.com*